10
BEST
TEACHING
PRACTICES

Third Edition

UNIVERSITY
OF THE FRASER VALLEY

*To my sons, Christopher Scott McBrayer and Kevin Lane McBrayer, and
in memory of their brother, Chad Michael McBrayer*

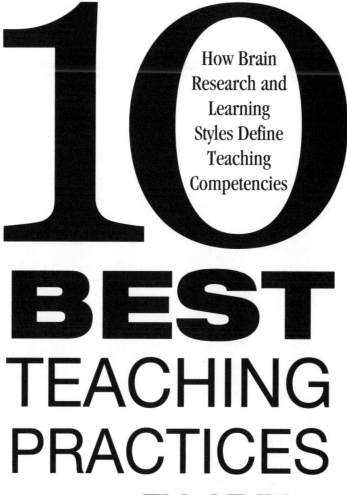

10

How Brain
Research and
Learning
Styles Define
Teaching
Competencies

BEST
TEACHING
PRACTICES

Third Edition

Donna Walker
Tileston

CORWIN
A SAGE Company

For information:

Corwin
A SAGE Company
2455 Teller Road
Thousand Oaks, California 91320
(800) 233-9936
Fax: (800) 417-2466
www.corwin.com

SAGE Ltd.
1 Oliver's Yard
55 City Road
London EC1Y 1SP
United Kingdom

SAGE Pvt. Ltd.
B 1/I 1 Mohan Cooperative
    Industrial Area
Mathura Road, New Delhi 110 044
India

SAGE Asia-Pacific Pte. Ltd.
33 Pekin Street #02-01
Far East Square
Singapore 048763

Printed in the United States of America

Library of Congress Cataloging-in-Publication Data

Tileston, Donna Walker.
Ten best teaching practices : how brain research and learning styles define teaching competencies / Donna Walker Tileston. — 3rd ed.
        p. cm.
Includes bibliographical references and index.
ISBN 978-1-4129-7393-9 (pbk.)
    1. Effective teaching—United States. 2. Learning. 3. Educational innovations—United States. 4. Educational change—United States. I. Title.

LB1775.2.T54 2011
371.102—dc22   2010042325

This book is printed on acid-free paper.

13 14 15 16 17 10 9 8 7 6 5 4 3 2

Acquisitions Editor:	Carol Collins
Associate Editor:	Megan Bedell
Editorial Assistant:	Sarah Bartlett
Production Editor:	Veronica Stapleton
Copy Editor:	Mark Bast
Typesetter:	C&M Digitals (P) Ltd.
Proofreader:	Susan Schon
Indexer:	Holly Day
Cover Designer:	Rose Storey
Permissions Editor:	Adele Hutchinson

Contents

Preface

When I first wrote this book, I said that we live in a time in which a revolution in education is occurring; that is still true, but it is now happening at warp speed. We are racing to keep up with advances in technology and new sciences such as neuroplasticity. For the first time in history students know how to use the technology of the classroom before their teachers—and, for the most part, they are better at it.

The faces of the classroom have changed dramatically from those of predominantly Anglo-Saxon background to a collage of cultures and races. Poverty is rampant in this country, and with it come all of the issues involved. The U.S. Census Bureau predicts that by 2024, the majority race in public schools will be Hispanic followed by African American. Given that national test scores tell us we're already doing a poor job of teaching English language learners, how effective will we be when they're the majority?

The information in this book has changed by at least 65 percent since the second edition in order to incorporate all the new research since 2005. It is important to note, however, that despite these rapid changes in our nation's classrooms and in our understanding of how the brain learns, the distillation of 10 basic best practices that I developed a decade ago has not changed. The implementation of these practices sometimes looks very different, involving new technologies, for instance, as well as strategies particularly designed to better incorporate English learners. But the essence of good teaching remains quite consistent. As I wrote in the first edition:

> I have identified 10 teaching practices that have tremendous power in the classroom when we incorporate the best of research with their implementation. These teaching strategies are based on the best research in the field and on real classroom experience by practitioners. More than 20 years ago, I began a dynamic field study on the factors that enhance learning and the factors that impede it. Along with a group of teachers, I used the research that was available at that time to help restructure a school in trouble. Positive results could be seen almost immediately and have been sustained over the years. Today, the school that once had low test scores, a high dropout rate, and many discipline problems enjoys some of

the highest test scores in the state, SAT and ACT scores well above the state and national average, and low incidences of discipline problems. What is significant about this study is that the results have been sustained over time—it was not a one-shot quick fix but a systemic process that has grown. The new research on how the brain learns has validated the structures that we put in place and built over the past two decades.

Chapter 1 looks at the importance of a climate that is enriched and emotionally supportive. As we examine the implications of cultures outside the dominant culture of the classroom, it has become evident that learners today need us to create a relationship first—before the substance of the learning. For some cultures such as African American it is essential that I build a relationship of trust first, especially if I am of a different culture. The new brain research on the effects of how students feel about the classroom and the learning as well as the brain's capacity to learn is critical. We now know that not only can we reverse the effects of an early negative environment, but, according to Sousa (2006), we can actually increase the IQ scores of students by as much as 20 points by enhancing the environment for learning. I consider this chapter to be critical, because if we cannot create a climate in which all students feel physically and emotionally secure, the rest doesn't matter.

Chapter 2 addresses the need for a wide repertoire of teaching techniques so that all students, regardless of how they learn best, will be successful. Schools of the past taught mainly to the auditory learners; schools of the future must teach to all learners. New research shows that as much as 80 percent to 90 percent of the classroom may be made up of students who don't learn auditorily (Sousa, 2006). We must examine not only the three most used modalities for incoming information, but the rhythm of the teaching as well. The attention span of the brain follows a rhythm that, if incorporated into the time frame of teaching, ensures greater response from students. Several years ago, I would have said that students from age 14 through adult will listen actively for 15 minutes before the brain begins to wander. Today, researchers such as Jensen (2010) tell us technology has narrowed down that time frame to about 10 minutes. To be effective teachers we must learn to use time as a tool that can be placed into teachable 10-minute segments with process skills utilized between.

Chapter 3 looks at the critical element of connections or transfers in learning. The brain is a seeker of connections, and where they do not exist, there seems to be a break in the learning while the brain creates a connection. Our job as educators is to build on connections that already exist and to help create connections where there are none. This chapter offers hope to the parents, teachers, and students as they search for ways to put learning into long-term memory. Since the last edition of this book, we have reexamined the idea of short-term and long-term memory. We now believe that there are two phases of short-term memory rather than just one and that each of those phases has a separate function and time clock in learning.

Chapter 4 is an investigation into the workings of the memory system. How does the brain decide what to toss and what to keep? More important, how can we take this new knowledge to the classroom? All of us, as educators, have experienced those agonizing moments when we realized that although we taught our hearts out, the students just didn't get it. With the mystery of how we learn and remember solved, teachers of the future have the opportunity to make learning more meaningful than at any other time in history. In this chapter we delve more deeply into what happens in the brain as our students make critical decisions about what is important to learn and what is not.

Chapter 5 looks at the need to provide motivating, challenging work in the classroom. Time is too precious a commodity to waste in the classroom. Our students will enter a world in which computers can do rote memory tasks. We must prepare them for the things computers cannot do—problem solving, complex thinking, and collaboration. We must see that every child—regardless of socioeconomic status—has access to a quality education. When students lack skills or have gaps in the learning then we must use scaffolding so that they can learn at a high level while we close the gaps.

Chapter 6 is a discussion of the power of true collaborative learning. In the global world, the need for articulation skills, the ability to work with a variety of people, and the ability to collaborate on problem solving is critical. One of the important skills of this century is the ability to talk to anyone, regardless of whether we agree with them or not (Pink, 2009). In a global world, people who can listen and who can seek to understand *why* are of great value.

Chapter 7 discusses the importance of success for all learners. We must take a hard look at student data in its desegregated form. We must look at cultural differences and the research on what works and what does not. It's time to bring in the experts and be honest about what is not working. Response to Intervention has the power to finally keep students from falling through the cracks and from being incorrectly placed in special education. It has the power but will not accomplish its goal unless we change the way we assess, the way we teach, and the way that we differentiate for culture.

Chapter 8 identifies what authentic assessment is and what it is not. Much is being written today about formative assessment and its role in helping all students to be successful. This chapter looks at some of the new research.

Chapter 9 looks at relevance as it applies to learning. Like climate, this is one of the most powerful areas of influence on how and whether the brain learns and remembers. It is the answer for those who ask, "When are we ever going to use this?" How can we take classroom skills to the real world, and how can we help students to see the possibilities?

Chapter 10 is a look into the future to an anytime, anywhere learning space. Technology is an integral part of the home and workplace. Technology is the tool of this century, just as a pen or pencil has been in former centuries. It should be an integral part of the classroom so that students don't have to "power down" when they come to school.

In Chapter 11, I provide some closing remarks based on the findings in this book and on the research from the school that we restructured more than 15 years ago. A true test for any restructured school is whether students are successful and, if so, whether they are successful over time. Students in our school began to show remarkable improvement almost immediately and have built on that success over time. When we began years ago to restructure this school, we did it based on the knowledge available at that time. We did not know many of the things that we now know about how the brain works; we applied what we knew worked for kids and then built on it as new information became available. Our instincts were correct. As these principles apply in that school, I believe they can apply in any school in the country.

PUBLISHER'S ACKNOWLEDGMENT

Corwin gratefully acknowledges the contributions of Beth Madison, Principal, George Middle School, Portland, Oregon.

About the Author

Donna Walker Tileston is a veteran teacher of three decades, a best-selling and award-winning author, and a full-time consultant. She is the president of Strategic Teaching & Learning, which provides services to schools throughout the United States, Canada, and worldwide. She is the author of more than 20 books, including *What Every Teacher Should Know: The 10-Book Collection* (Corwin, 2004), which won the Association of Educational Publishers' 2004 Distinguished Achievement Award as a Professional Development Handbook. She has also written the following for Corwin:

Closing the Poverty and Culture Gap: Strategies to Reach Every Student (2009)

Teaching Strategies That Prepare Students for High-Stakes Tests (2008)

Teaching Strategies for Active Learning: Five Essentials for Your Teaching Plan (2007)

What Every Parent Should Know About Schools, Standards, and High-Stakes Tests (2006)

Ten Best Teaching Practices: How Brain Research, Learning Styles, and Standards Define Teaching Competencies, Second Edition (2005)

Training Manual for What Every Teacher Should Know (2005)

What Every Teacher Should Know About Learning, Memory, and the Brain (2004)

What Every Teacher Should Know About Diverse Learners (2004)

What Every Teacher Should Know About Instructional Planning (2004)

What Every Teacher Should Know About Effective Teaching Strategies (2004)

What Every Teacher Should Know About Classroom Management and Discipline (2004)

What Every Teacher Should Know About Student Assessment (2004)

What Every Teacher Should Know About Special Learners (2004)

What Every Teacher Should Know About Media and Technology (2004)

What Every Teacher Should Know About the Profession and Politics of Teaching (2004)

What Every Teacher Should Know: The 10-Book Collection (2004)

Strategies for Teaching Differently: On the Block or Not (1998)

She received her bachelor's degree from The University of North Texas, her master's from East Texas State University, and her doctorate from Texas A&M University, Commerce. She may be reached at www.wetsk.com.

Creating an Environment That Facilitates Learning

The difference between an expectation and a standard is that the standard is the bar, and the expectation is our belief about whether students will ever reach the bar.

—Robyn R. Jackson

In the first edition of this book, I wrote the following lines about creating a classroom environment that is conducive to learning. I repeat them here because the importance of this aspect of learning remains paramount to the craft of teaching:

> An enriched and supportive environment is so important that none of the other techniques discussed will be really effective unless the issues of enrichment and support are addressed first. In a world full of broken relationships, broken promises, and broken hearts, a strong supportive relationship is important to students. While we cannot control the students' environments outside the classroom, we have tremendous control over their environment for seven hours each day. We have the power to create positive or negative images about education, to develop an enriched environment, and

to become the catalysts for active learning. We now know that how we feel about education has great impact on how the brain reacts to it. Emotion and cognitive learning are not separate entities; they work in tandem with one another. (Tileston, 2005, p. 1)

Ask teachers what is keeping them from being the kind of teacher they dreamed of being and you will probably get an answer that involves the motivation level or lack thereof demonstrated by their students. Through current brain research, we know so much more now about what causes us to be motivated to learn and to complete tasks at a high level. In his groundbreaking book *Drive*, Daniel Pink (2009) surprises us with what current brain research says about what really motivates our students and us. In the last century we relied on the carrot-and-stick approach to motivating our students. We offered tangible rewards for finished work and behavior such as stickers, free time, prizes, and even money. Pink says that in this day and time what truly motivates us clusters around three things: (1) autonomy, (2) mastery, and (3) purpose.

THE NEED FOR AUTONOMY IN THE CLASSROOM

We seem to be hardwired to be active, engaged, and curious. Pink (2009) calls this our default switch, and he adds that when we reach a point in our lives—whether it is in middle school or middle age—that we are not curious and actively engaged in learning, it is because something has turned the switch to the "off" position. Watch a two-year-old at play if you have any doubts about these phenomena of natural curiosity. We help build autonomy or self-direction in our students through task, time, technique, and team.

Task: When possible, give students choices in how they demonstrate understanding, the independent projects that they work on, and in how they tackle procedural tasks. Provide the parameters and the scaffolding needed and then stand back and let students work on the tasks. In the last century we were so fixed on a model from industry that compartmentalized and standardized everything that even elementary-classroom art projects became cookie cutter works. This century is about creativity, and it is time to throw away the cookie cutters.

Time: Time is the brutal enemy of understanding in the classroom. We live by a set of standards that must be taught in a given amount of time—and too often it is time that rules how and what we teach, rather than student success and understanding. What if we got rid of this "tail wagging the dog" idea and began to believe and implement a system that allowed students more time if they needed it or wanted it to create a better product? What if we put the emphasis on the quality of the learning rather than on just covering the subject? What if we looked at progress over time rather than time over progress?

Technique: Autonomy over technique refers to providing choices to students when they do group or individual projects and when they demonstrate understanding. To the extent possible, allow students to show that they understand through a variety of ways such as written or verbal projects, demonstrations, models, or using a kinesthetic or other creative approach of their own. In my workshops I often use the following problem to demonstrate this technique: *There are 100 people in a room. If everyone in the room shakes hands with everyone else, how many handshakes is this?* For the verbal learners, there is a formula; for the visual learners, they can draw or use graphics to show the answer; and for the kinesthetic learners, they can demonstrate the answer.

Team: Autonomy over teams occurs when I allow students to create social networks of their own choosing to study together, complete projects together, and to collaborate. As technology becomes available to each student, those networks can go beyond the classroom. For example, a small group is working on an independent project in the form of a book report using technology. The group might want to add to their team a teacher or peer who has used this method successfully online or a consultant from one of the universities where this technique has been developed. There are places right now where students are doing this—where learning is not limited by the classroom teacher or by the bricks and mortar of a school building—and it adds great depth to the project. Jensen (1997) says that the best learning state for students is one in which there is mild stress—pushing the envelope slightly. In this state, students feel a nudge, but they have the knowledge base to be successful. In other words, when we push the envelope we need to be sure that our students have the foundation and the tools to be successful otherwise it becomes a high-stress situation in which none of us do our best work. Pink (2009) sums up autonomy with an important statement to those of us who value accountability:

> Motivation 2.0 assumed that if people had freedom, they would shirk—and that autonomy was a way to bypass accountability. Motivation 3.0 begins with a different assumption. It presumes that people want to be accountable—and that making sure they have control over their task, their time, their technique, and their team is a pathway to that destination. (p. 107)

STUDENTS' STATES OF MIND: MAKING LEARNING POSITIVE

Have you ever been so involved in a project that you literally lost track of time? You were completely engaged and were seeking mastery. Psychologist Csikszentmihalyi, as discussed by Pink (2009, p. 114), was curious as to what was going on in the brains of people while they were totally engaged in what they were doing. He found that people who are engaged, whether it is in learning or a project, are in a state of flow. It is the state of flow of the brain that causes us to pay attention, finish work at a high level, or sleep through class.

Our brains are constantly changing their emotional states (flow) based on both internal and external stimuli. Jensen (2003) explains these states as patterns in the brain that affect our behaviors. These patterns shift constantly as new stimuli change them. For example, a student may be listening to the teacher when a fight erupts in the hallway. Suddenly, her state has changed from attentive learner to one characterized by very different emotions such as excitement, disgust, anger, or sadness. The kinds of states that students bring to the classroom depend, in part, on the states that are dominant or most often used by them outside the classroom. We all have attractor states and repeller states.

Signature states or attractor states are the states that we enter most often. These neural networks have been strengthened over time through the emotions and sensations attached to that particular state. Jensen (2003) explains,

> Some people laugh a lot because that's their primary attractor state. Others are angry a lot—that's their strongest attractor state. That state becomes their allostatic (adjusted stress load) state, instead of the healthier homeostatic state. The result is that they will often pick fights with others just to feel "like themselves" by reentering that familiar state. (p. 9)

States make up our personalities and can usually be predicted based on past experience. By the same token, our states in regard to learning are created by the experiences that we have most often in the classroom. If I experience failure, ridicule, embarrassment, or even fear in the classroom most often, then my state in that classroom will be based on avoiding those things. Repeller states are those states that we avoid, states that we experience only for short periods or in extremes. A student might experience failure in math and success in all other subjects; that experience will lead to a state for learning in all other classes except math. Jensen (2003) adds,

> Our systems naturally repel these states when we move towards them. We tend to avoid them because the complex interplay of our intent (frontal lobes) and the myriad of our other subsystems (emotions, hunger, high-low energy cycles, heart rate, etc.) indicate that we'll find no good maintaining in those states. (p.10)

Students enter our classrooms with a great deal going on in the brain that has nothing to do with the learning at hand. They may have had an argument at home before school or a negative experience in the hallway. They may be excited about an upcoming event or a new boyfriend or girlfriend. As teachers, we have a great deal of competition for our students' attention. Learning is the "process by which our system memorizes these neuronal assemblies (our states) until they become attractor states"

(Jensen, 2003, p. 10). What if students do not have attractor states about learning but have, over time, created a pattern for repelling the learning? We can guide them to a state in which learning is an attractor state. By using what we know about the brain and what attracts the brain to learning, we can, over time, reverse the state of mind of our students.

In order to bring students to mastery, we need to understand how to bring them to engagement in the learning. True mastery is a process of constantly moving past my "personal best." What was my personal best in second-grade mathematics will not be good enough in third-grade mathematics. I am constantly trying to achieve greater heights. It is no surprise that during the winter Olympics, we constantly heard the words, "He has a new personal best with that score." If I want students in my classroom to achieve mastery, I must help them to create personal goals for the learning, and I need to revisit those goals often to help my students see their progress. Most students have not been directly taught how to follow through when there are constraints to meeting their goals. Thus, they often throw up their hands and simply give up at the first sign of trouble. We can help our students to achieve mastery by teaching them positive self-talk; show them what you do when you cannot get a problem solved or how you determine the meaning of a new word in a sentence. In a study on why some cadets in military academies drop out and some stay regardless of circumstances (Duckworth, Peterson, Matthews, & Kelly, 2007), researchers found that those who stayed with the program in spite of grueling and tough training were those who had a "grit," the ability to effectively monitor and regroup when they were having difficulty with meeting long-term goals.

Most of us were taught to begin our teaching with the cognitive center of the brain. It is no wonder that teachers all over the country lament the fact that students are not motivated to learn. We know from researchers such as Marzano and Kendall (2008) that motivation to learn is controlled by the self-system of the brain, not the cognitive system. Let me say that again: all learning begins in the self-system of the brain. It is this system that decides whether the student will pay attention and engage in the learning; it is the learning state that most of us seek in our classrooms. Marzano (2001a) puts it this way:

> The self-system consists of an interrelated system of attitudes, beliefs, and emotions. It is the interaction of these attitudes, beliefs, and emotions that determines both motivation and attention. Specifically, the self-system determines whether an individual will engage in or disengage in a given task; it also determines how much energy the individual will bring to the given task. (p.50)

Once the decision has been made to pay attention or begin a task, the metacognitive system of the brain takes over and makes a plan for carrying out the work. Only then is the cognitive system employed. Figure 1.1 is a graphic representation of this process.

Figure 1.1   The Systems of Thinking

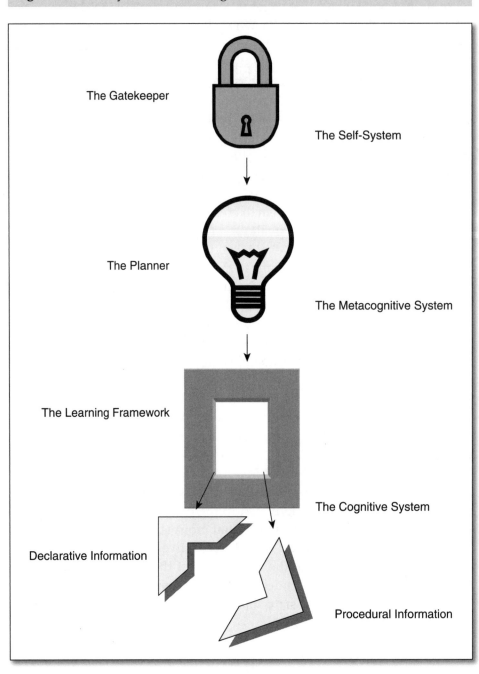

As teachers, we need to be cognizant of the fact that the decision whether or not to engage in the learning is going to take place with or without us. We can influence that decision by the way we approach the teaching and learning process. We also can influence the learning state of our students through what we say and do. Jensen (2003, p. 11) says that we should target the state that we want for our students depending on the learning activity. He lists the states based on the amount of energy they require from highest need for energy to lowest need:

1. Hyper, overactive

2. Physically active, learning

3. Writing or talking

4. Focused thinking

5. Alert concentration

6. Scattered thinking

7. Visualizing

8. Relaxed focus

9. Daydreaming

10. Drowsy, drifting

The following three criteria are critical to the decision by the brain to pay attention to the learning (see Tileston, 2004a).

1. The Personal Importance of the Learning to the Student

No one will argue that learning is important. However, for learning to be addressed by the brain, it must be perceived as important to the individual. The first criterion is that the student must believe the learning satisfies a personal need or goal. Marzano (2001a) explains it this way: "What an individual considers to be important is probably a function of the extent to which it meets one of two conditions: it is perceived as instrumental in satisfying a basic need, or it is perceived as instrumental in the attainment of a personal goal." Jensen (2010) reinforces the importance of goal setting as a way to emphasize the personal importance of the new learning to students. Jensen suggests,

> Encourage students to set daily, weekly, and long-term goals. Check in with them on a regular basis, provide feedback, and validate their progress. For example, ask students to share their goals with classmates by posting them as timelines or charts. Public recognition is a great motivator and strategy for reinforcing progress. Once distressed learners set a goal, do everything in your power to help them succeed. (p. 68)

How many of us have heard students say, "When are we ever going to use this?" Students today are in information overload; if they only need to know it for the test on Friday, then they will memorize it long enough to put it on the test and then promptly forget it. If it has real-world meaning to them personally, it is more likely to be placed into long-term memory. Begin units of study by helping students see the importance of the learning to them personally. In his book, *The Art and Science of Teaching: A Comprehensive Framework for Effective Instruction* (2007), Marzano cites a meta-analysis by Lipsey and Wilson (1993) in which 204 studies are synthesized to determine the effect size of setting goals. An effect size provides us with data on the effect of using a particular instructional strategy as opposed to classrooms where the strategy is not being used. We can ask the question, "If I use this strategy in my classroom, what will be the average effect on student learning? In this case the effect size was 0.55. This means that in the 204 studies they examined, the average score in classes where goal setting was effectively employed was 0.55 standard deviations greater than the average score in classes where goal setting was not employed" (Marzano, 2007, p. 11). Effect sizes can be interpreted as percentile gains as well. In this case, when goals and objectives were set for the learning, the average gain in learning was 21 percentile points. Think about your classroom: would this be significant to the learning of your students?

Personal importance may be viewed in many ways. Some examples include the following:

- *Personal goals that address immediate needs.* For example, if students from the inner city learn basic math facts, this will help prevent them from being cheated on the street. Another example would be a student who is about to take an exam for advanced credit. This student is more apt to pay attention to learning that will help him or her prepare for the qualifying test.
- *Personal goals that increase the esteem of the student to a particular group.* For example, a student who wants to impress friends or gain the attention or affection of parents or of a school group will pay more attention to those topics that are of importance to the other individuals or groups.
- *Personal goals that are long term.* For example, students may not see the relevance of studying slope in their immediate lives but may realize that they must know this information to get into a higher-math class later on. Another student may want to work in international finance and thus sees the importance of learning about the cultures of other countries.

We might want to specifically ask our students why something might be important to know or do. Marzano and Kendall (2008, p. 148) provide these question stems for the teacher:

How important is it to you?

Why do you think it might be important?

Can you provide some reasons why it is important?

How logical is your thinking?

2. The Development of Self-Efficacy in the Learner

The second criterion that is examined by the brain is called *self-efficacy*. Self-efficacy differs from self-esteem in that self-esteem is based on a feeling or belief about oneself that may or may not have been proved. I may believe that I can do the work even though I have never tried it before. While this is important, self-efficacy is more powerful because it is based on fact: I know that I can do the more difficult math assignment because I have had success with math before. This is one of the reasons why it is so important for students to experience success—even incremental success—in the classroom. Success really does breed success.

Self-efficacy is also the belief that one has the capacity to be successful. Capacity is based on ability, resources, and power over the situation. A student may believe that he or she can do the math assignment but may not have enough directions (resources) to carry it out. Many students will give up at this point. Another example would be a student who believes that he or she has the ability and the resources but cannot complete the assignment because the home environment does not allow him or her to work. While we cannot change the home environment, we can help provide a place to work. Some of the ways that the classroom teacher can build self-efficacy include the following:

- *Provide opportunities for success.* This does not mean "watering down the information." Giving students an inferior education does not build self-esteem or self-efficacy. Give students the capacity to be successful and then provide feedback often. Feedback should include both positive reinforcement (what they are doing correctly) and suggestions for improvement as needed. Just saying "good job" is not feedback. Build into units an opportunity to celebrate success. Jensen (2010) says, "Little rituals, such as celebrating the completion of a new unit with a group success chant, can go a long way toward warming the classroom climate and reinforcing positive accomplishments" (p. 68).
- *Build capacity in students by providing adequate directions and opportunities to practice the learning.* Be sure that there is adequate time for the learning to take place and that students have been given feedback.
- *Encourage students to develop their own goals for the learning.* Do this by modeling. Place your goals for the learning in the classroom so that students can see the goals. Go back to the goals often so that students can see their progress. For nonreaders, use symbols for the learning and send the unit objectives home to parents. Post learning goals on the Internet or intranet at your learning site.
- *Provide students with the expectations for the learning up front, before the learning begins.* Do this in writing when possible. The expectations might be in the form of a matrix or rubric, or they might simply be written out and given to the learners. By doing this, teachers get rid of the "gotchas," in which students are assessed for something that they did not learn.

3. How Students Feel About the Learning, Classroom, Subject Matter, and Other Students

If you have ever been in a classroom in which the emotional climate was one of tension or fear, you already know why the third criterion, how students feel about the learning, is so important. Our species has survived because our brains attend to information by priority. If we are under threat, whether physical, emotional, or otherwise, our brain pays attention to the threat over all other incoming stimuli. As Jensen (1997) says, "The brain stem is the part of the brain that directs your behavior under negative stress; and is the most responsive to any threat. When threat is perceived, excessive cortisol is released into the body causing higher-order thinking to take a backseat to automatic functions that may help you survive." Goleman (1995), in his book *Emotional Intelligence*, talks about the effects of stress over time. He says that when an individual is under stress he or she cannot remember, learn, or make decisions clearly because "stress makes us stupid."

Not all of these criteria are equal in weight. For example, a student may not see the importance of learning about slope in mathematics but likes the class, respects the teacher, and has had positive experiences in math in the past, and so the student may choose to give the subject a chance to prove to himself or herself that it is relevant. Marzano (2001a) says, "If the task is judged important, if the probability of success is high, and if positive affect is generated or associated with the task, the individual will be motivated to engage in the new task. If the new task is evaluated as having low relevance and/or low probability of success and has an associated negative effect, motivation to engage in the task is low."

Figure 1.2 is a graphic model that depicts, in simple terms, the decision-making process going on in the brain during the self-system phase of the learning.

An important aspect of student motivation in a diverse classroom is whether the teacher has made the classroom and the learning culturally responsive. Students who come from a culture that respects and edifies the efforts of the group may feel very uncomfortable in our typical individualistic and competitive classrooms. Zeichner (2003) discusses the culturally responsive instructural program:

> Culturally responsive instruction contains two critical elements: first, the incorporation of aspects of students' languages, cultures, daily experiences into the academic and social context of schooling; and second, the explicit teaching of the school's codes and customs (for example, the culture of the classroom) so that students will be able to participate fully in the social dynamic of the classroom. (p. 101)

We may need to identify and teach to a dual-culture mode in which we honor the culture of the students while helping them to understand the dominant culture and the differences.

Figure 1.2 Depiction of the Self-System of the Brain

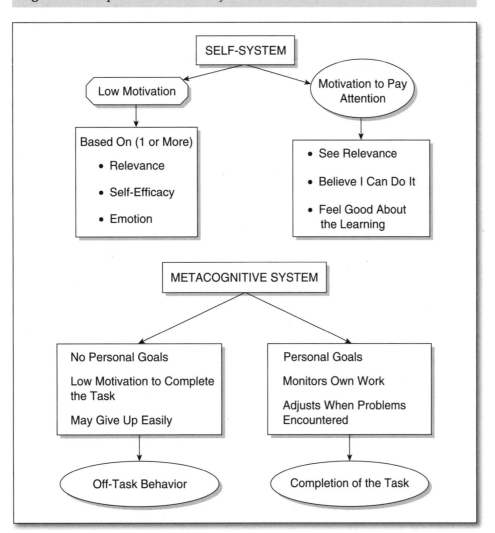

Although a goal in education is to promote learning, sometimes outside factors inhibit the process. One of these inhibitors is stress, and a common reason for stress in students is threat. Jensen (1998) says, "Threat impairs brain cells. Threat also changes the body's chemistry and impacts learning." Stress chemicals act on the hippocampus, the part of the brain that filters and helps store long-term factual memories. Some examples of threat in the classroom include anything that embarrasses a student, unrealistic deadlines, a student's inability to speak a language, inappropriate learning styles, and an uncomfortable classroom culture (Jensen, 2010).

Years ago, I was involved in a restructuring project in a high school that proved to me the enormous impact of positive climate on student learning. Our faculty had come to a point of desperation: we knew students were not learning at a quality level, and we knew they did not want to come to school. Our high dropout rate was proof. We understood how the students felt because we too were burned out. Our test scores were average at best;

in addition to the high dropout rate, we had a fledgling attendance rate and discipline problems. So we came together and made a list of all the things we thought were wrong with the school and the things that were keeping it from being the kind of learning place we wanted it to be. We did our homework. We studied the research and called in the experts. We were actively involved in more than 15 days of training on the factors that enhance learning and those that impede it. As we came to know more about how children learn, we changed our attitude about teaching and learning, and we reinvented our school into the kind of place we believed school should be.

When our students came back in the fall, it was to an entirely different kind of school. On the first day of school, we stood in front of our classes and gave students a pep talk that would make any coach proud. We talked about how we believed in our students. We encouraged them to do their best work, and we promised them that we would be the best teachers we had ever been. We told them that there would be no more "gotchas" in our school; that they would always be told what they needed to do to be successful in our classrooms—and if they did it, they would be successful. We quit teaching as if we were the all-knowing scribes and made the students active participants in the learning. We created real-world applications to the learning and told students up front what the learning had to do with their world. We encouraged creativity, connections to the learning, and reflective thinking. We created a place where learning was respected and nourished—and we all thrived.

In October of that year, we gave our state exam, which students must pass in order to graduate. As a faculty, we told ourselves not to be discouraged if the scores were not improved over the prior year. After all, we had been teaching differently for only two months, and there was no way we could make up for the lack of knowledge in such a short time. When the scores came back, there was so much improvement that we thought it was a fluke. In the past, only 28 percent of our at-risk students had mastered every part of the test on the first try. When our tests came back, 67 percent of our at-risk students mastered every part of the state test. We were baffled. We knew we could not have taught these students that much material in only two months!

That winter, I attended a seminar on brain research conducted by the late Madeline Hunter. She talked first about the research of the 1970s regarding something called the *placebo effect*, in which a group of people were told that they were being given penicillin for a virus when, in fact, they were being given a placebo. Regardless, one-third of them got well. Her new research showed that if the doctor giving the placebo believes that he is giving the group penicillin, and if he convinces the group of this, more than half of them will get well. I knew then what had happened to our at-risk students. For the first time, as a group, we believed that all kids could learn; we convinced the students of that fact, and more than half of them—67 percent—"got well." What a powerful influence emotion is on the brain. When we begin to tap into that power in schools, remarkable things are possible.

In his book *How the Brain Learns*, David Sousa (2006) talks about the importance of emotion on the brain. He says that emotional responses can actually diminish the brain's ability to process cognitive information:

> We have all had experiences when anger, fear of the unknown, or joy quickly overcame our rational thoughts. This override of conscious thought can be strong enough to cause temporary inability to talk . . . or move. This happens because the hippocampus is susceptible to stress hormones which can inhibit cognitive functioning and long-term memory.

Students who feel threatened in the classroom, whether physically or emotionally, are operating in a survival mode, and while learning can take place in that mode, it is with much difficulty. If a student feels that no matter what he does he can never please the teacher, if a student feels that no matter how hard she tries she can never understand the subject—whether the threat is real or perceived—that student will not ever be able to reach his or her potential in that environment.

BUILDING A BRAIN-FRIENDLY ENVIRONMENT

While we cannot control the lives of our students outside the classroom, as teachers, we can provide a quality environment for them each day. We do this by ensuring that the environment within our classrooms is enriched (meaningful, active engagement) and supportive. Factors that help create an enriched and supportive environment include the following: a sense of belonging, a high level of support for achievement, a sense of empowerment, more on-ramps, an advocate for every student, and resiliency in students.

A Sense of Belonging

All of us want to belong somewhere. We want to feel we are a part of the experience and that we are accepted. When students do not feel accepted, for whatever reason, they are more likely to find negative places to belong. That is what helps keep gangs active in our students' lives. Gangs and other negative influences fill a need that so often is not met in positive settings. As educators, we must create an environment in which students feel safe and accepted, an environment in which we are all learners together and where we feel a sense of togetherness—one where there are no "gotchas." Students are told up front what they must do to be successful, and then we must be faithful and hold them only to the criteria that we set.

Give students the tools they need to be successful and then allow them the opportunity to fulfill that success. I have never met a student who wanted to fail. Hanson and Childs (1998) published the results of a survey given to students in Chicago, Houston, and Norfolk that asked what most concerned them about school. The number-one concern (51.77%) was school failure. We have the power to elevate or eliminate that concern.

A High Level of Support for Achievement

Teachers and students expect quality work; they will not accept anything less. We insult students when we accept mediocre work. Students are given very clear directions about what they must do to be successful, they are given the tools they need in order to make that success possible, and they are given the time to do it right. The expectation is consistent throughout the school; students cannot turn in shoddy work in one classroom and then be expected to do their best in another. A friend of mine who is a powerful math teacher has a sign in her room that says, "I promise to be the best math teacher you have ever had. Will you promise to be the best math student you have ever been?" Students who have never before been successful in mathematics are successful in her classroom. It's a matter of attitude.

In the last century a common slogan given to teachers was "fake it before you make it." The slogan was an effort to lead teachers to at least pretend they believed that all kids can learn, with the idea that students would prove it true. Jackson says (2009, p. 81), "The problem with this approach is that if you only adjust your behavior without first changing your perspective, sooner or later, your true expectations will leak through. Because an expectation is a belief that something will happen, our behavior will reveal what you truly believe." Another example of the difference between truly believing and providing lip service is in the way that we work with students who do not look like us. So many times teachers will say that they are color-blind and treat all students the same. Yet visits to their classroom often tell a different story as the materials, the things on the walls, and the teacher-made materials are all of people who are the same as the teacher. There is a huge difference between being politically correct and providing a culturally responsive classroom. As Jackson (2009, p. 82) says, "Our expectations are the intersection between what we believe about our teaching situation and our own abilities to handle it and what we believe is important. We can only have high expectations of our students if we believe that it is possible that we can help our students and if we believe that it is important to do so."

A Sense of Empowerment

All of us feel better about our circumstances when we feel we have some power over what happens to us. Students should have input into the decisions that affect their lives daily. Look at the policies and rules in your school and ask, "How many are necessary, and how many no longer apply but are in place because at some point in the past they were deemed necessary?" In the school that we changed so dramatically, we rebuilt our list of rules from zero based on the true needs of the students, staff, and community for that time. It was amazing how many rules were on the books simply because, over time, no one had bothered to ask if they were really necessary. Hanson and Childs (1998) say, "In a school with a positive climate, policies encourage and seek a win/win result." Covey (1989) describes win/win as "a frame of mind and heart that constantly seeks mutual benefit in all human interactions. A win/win solution means that all parties feel good about the decision and feel committed to the action plan. Win/win sees life as a cooperative, not a competitive arena." In the classroom, we empower students when we involve them in the class rules and when we give them choices in the assignments. As a matter of fact, anytime we give students choices, we give them power.

In our restructured high school, I saw an amazing application of this principle of giving students choices. We had a nagging problem with discipline; there were fights in the hallway every day. Our schedule included a 15-minute activity period designed to give students a chance to go to the library, go by a teacher's room to leave an assignment, or just to give the students a break to have a soft drink and to speak to their friends. Students loved it; we hated it. That was the time when we had the largest number of individual discipline problems. Out of frustration, the principal took the 15-minute break out of the daily schedule.

A group of students, appointed by the general student body, visited the principal to see if there was any way they could get their break time back into the schedule. The principal told them that he would make a deal with them: as long as there were no fights, no acts of vandalism of school property, and no litter after break or lunch, they could have the break. However, anytime an adult had to break up a fight, anytime there was an act of vandalism, and anytime the hallway was left with debris after break they would lose break for three days. Signs in the hallway informed students whether break was on for the day or not. Over time, there was a dramatic change in the students' behavior; they patrolled between classes and before and after school, and the difference in the school was remarkable. For some students, the 15-minute break was the only time during the school day that they saw their boyfriends or girlfriends. One afternoon, I was seated in one of the student's desks waiting for the bell to ring when I heard a commotion outside the door. There were no teachers in sight, and no one knew I was there. Two students were getting ready to fight. They were glaring at each other and mouthing off. The tension was high. Before I could get to the hallway, between 10 and 15 students had gotten between the angry students, pushing them back, talking to them, cooling them off—much the way pro athletes do in a game where a penalty would be crucial. This became the norm in that school, and over time discipline problems became minimal.

More On-Ramps

Schools provide plenty of opportunities for students to drop out—physically, mentally, or both. Metaphorically, these are the off-ramps. What we need are more on-ramps to keep students engaged, in school, and on track. First, schools can provide more on-ramps by providing more choices in offerings, including not only high-level courses that prepare for higher education but current, meaningful studies that lead to vocations. Take a hard look at the course offerings and ask some critical questions. What do students really need to know and be able to do in order to have marketable skills? Is there a segment of the school population that is being left out? Could we team up with community colleges and major universities to provide more opportunities for our students? Why can't students take courses in high school that will help them complete two-year associate degree programs? As a matter of fact, most of those courses could be taught through collaborative efforts with colleges and universities so that students could leave high school with most of the coursework completed. With video-conferencing and distance-learning capabilities, students can complete high school and some college work prior to graduation.

Second, we provide on-ramps when we provide choices within the curriculum that incorporate learning styles and multiple intelligences in the process. Independent projects are a primary opportunity to give students choices for products. The teacher who sets the criteria for the work in the class, yet provides choices within that work, does not diminish the quality of the work but enhances the depth of the learning by giving students opportunities to bring a variety of products to the learning. Because students learn in different modalities—kinesthetic, auditory, and visual—teachers who use a variety of techniques provide more opportunities for success to their students.

Third, schools provide on-ramps when they lead students to know that if they fail, if they make a mistake, if they break a rule, they can overcome it. I am convinced that we could save quite a few students if they knew that a mistake does not mean there is no hope. While I believe that we need to be accountable for the things we do, I also believe that we must not take away a student's hope that he or she can overcome whatever problem is in the way.

An Advocate for Every Student

I taught in an inner-city high school of 3,000 students in a non–air conditioned Texas classroom on the third floor. Hardly a day went by without some act of violence, whether it was a student beaten up, a robbery, or slashed tires in the parking lot. I loved my kids; they made tremendous sacrifices just to come to school each day. I learned far more from them than they probably learned from me. One important rule I learned in that environment was that every kid needs an advocate. All kids need to know that someone is looking over their shoulder and knows whether they have been absent too much, whether they are in danger of failure, whether they are on track for graduation, and if they are having problems in the classroom. We know now that the small-school concept is better because it provides the opportunity for teachers and administration to get to know the students personally. Not all of us are in a position to work and learn in small schools, however. In the age of megaschools, there are some creative solutions to providing the small-school experience within the large-school building. Academic teaming, in which teams of teachers are responsible for 100 or fewer students, is one way that we have been able to provide the advocacy needed by students. Under this model, teams meet on a regular weekly, if not daily, basis. Part of the responsibility of the team is to check on the 100 students assigned to see who has been absent too much, who is tardy often, who is a discipline problem, and who is in danger of failure. This team provides support and counseling to these students on an individual basis. The team may meet with other teachers, administrators, support staff, and/or parents on the student's behalf.

Another popular variation of this is the teacher-mentor who is assigned from 20 to 25 students for whom he or she is responsible throughout their school years on that campus. In elementary school, these are often called *homeroom teachers*; at the secondary level, they take on other titles, but the concept is the same. In high school, the teacher-mentor stays with the same students throughout high school and may take on some of the duties of school orientation with the group. These teachers are critical to setting a positive school climate for the students to whom they are assigned.

As we move to a very diverse population, this is especially important in helping to give all students survival skills. Werner and Smith (1992) cite Rutter, who talks about the needs of at-risk children and suggests, "If we want to help vulnerable youngsters we need to focus on the protective processes that bring about changes in life trajectories from risk to adaptation." Rutter includes among them (a) those that reduce the risk impact; (b) those that reduce the likelihood of negative chain reactions; (c) those that promote self-esteem and self-efficacy; and (d) those that open up opportunities. Werner and Smith (1992) explain, "We have seen these processes at work among the resilient children in our study and among those youths that recovered from serious coping problems in young adulthood. They represent the essence of any effective intervention program, whether by professionals or volunteers."

Resiliency in Students

Bonnie Benard has been one of the most outspoken authors in the field of building resiliency in children. Using a paraphrase of Benard's definition of resiliency (2003), we might say that resiliency is the ability to succeed in spite of adverse circumstances. Some of the factors that seem to be paramount to building resiliency in children include the following:

1. The teacher
   o Outside of the family, one of the most powerful influences on children is the caring teacher (Benard, 2003).

2. High expectations
   o As we have already discussed, truly believing that students can meet the expectations of the classroom is important. Benard (2003) says that in addition, teachers with high expectations help their students to not take personally the adversity around them, to understand that adversity is not permanent, and to understand that when we have setbacks they are not pervasive.

3. Moving from a deficit model

   o Build on student strengths first rather than looking at children as needing to be fixed. Give them a voice in the classroom and listen to them. I love the story that Bonnie Benard tells about a successful teacher who said if you really listen to your students, they will tell you how to teach them.

In their book, *Resiliency in Schools: Making It Happen for Students and Educators*, Henderson and Milstein (2003) list the following characteristics of families, schools, communities, and peer groups that foster resiliency. They

- promote close bonds;
- value and encourage education;
- use a high-warmth/low-criticism style of interaction;
- set and enforce clear boundaries (rules, norms, and laws);
- encourage supportive relationships with many caring others;
- promote sharing of responsibilities, service to others, "required helpfulness";
- provide access to resources for basic needs of housing, employment, health care, and recreation;
- express high, realistic expectations for success;
- encourage goal setting and mastery;
- encourage prosocial development of values (like altruism) and life skills (like cooperation);
- provide leadership, decision-making, and other opportunities for meaningful participation;
- and appreciate the unique talents of each individual.

Although we cannot ensure that students have that kind of support outside the school, we have tremendous power to see that they have that support for seven hours each day.

MEASURING SUCCESS

We have looked at effect sizes of the instructional strategies tied to motivation as well. It is important to note here a warning from Marzano (2007) about expecting good results without high-quality effort and implementation attached to them: "Educators must remember that the goal-setting strategy and every other strategy mentioned in this book must be done well and at the right time to produce positive effects on student learning" (p. 12). The best instructional strategy in the world will only bring the desired results when it is executed correctly. Figure 1.3 shows some of the ways that positive environments can be measured and the indicators of success.

Figure 1.3 Indicators of an Environment That Facilitates Learning

Assessment Tool	Indicators of Success
Matrix/rubric	Higher degree of success by students overall
Climate surveys	Results show a high satisfaction with school, low stress level, and a belief that grades, assignments, and assessments are fair and equitable.
Overall failure rate	Declining
Attendance rates	Rising
Dropout rates	Low; anything higher than zero is not acceptable
Discipline referrals	Declining
Course offerings	A wide variety of options that include flexible scheduling where appropriate
Teaching methods	Include visual, tactile, and auditory tools
Differentiation	The background knowledge of students is an integral part of the teaching and learning process.

CONCLUSION

As we acknowledge that all learning begins in the self-system of the brain, we must utilize processes in the classroom that help facilitate self-efficacy, a positive climate, and an adequate challenge so that our students are motivated to learn. Although teachers cannot motivate students directly (motivation comes from within the individual), we can create a climate that nurtures the processes that affect motivation. Namely, we can create a moderate-stress (some stress in the learning prevents boredom), high-challenge environment that is realistic in its goals for attainment and supportive of building the infrastructure to be successful. New research such as that from Pink (2009) indicates that the motivation in all of us is triggered by the opportunity for autonomy, the tools to create mastery, and by finding purpose in the learning. As teachers, we can provide the scaffolding (structures) necessary for our students to be successful and help lead them to mastery. We can move away from the cookie cutter approach to learning to allow students some autonomy in their learning.

Differentiating for Different Learning Styles

Help students understand how they learn best. Give them an assessment that helps them discover their multiple intelligences or preferred learning modality. Then show them how to use this information to prevent the difficulty of assignments not matched to their learning style or preferred modality, how to seek help, and how to adapt their studying, note taking, and even the learning task itself to better meet their learning needs.

—R. R. Jackson

We now know that some of the concepts that we held about the brain in the last century were not true. For example, we once believed that intelligence was fixed and could not be changed. Thanks to new and emerging research, we now know that our intelligence changes throughout our lives. True, we are born into this world with about half of our neurological wiring in place. This is one of the reasons we have survived as a species; it is this wiring that allows us to breathe, eat, drink, swallow, learn a language, and take in our world. But as Jensen (2006, pp. 8–9) puts it, "These connections ensure that the infant can eat, breath and respond to the environment. But they are not fixed; some will die from disuse and others will flourish with constant usage. Brains will produce new neurons, lose neurons, make connections and lose other connections, all based on our experience." Or as Doidge (2007) writes, "Neuroplastic research has shown us that every sustained activity ever mapped—including physical activities, sensory activities, learning, thinking, and imaging—changes the brain as well as the mind" (p. 288). This neurological pruning takes place throughout our lives depending on our interests, health, and willingness to learn.

We know that about 98 percent of all new learning enters the brain through the senses (Jensen, 1997)—primarily through visual, tactile, and auditory experiences. (Taste and smell are also useful avenues for learning but are not often used in the classroom.) Most of us have a preference for how we learn. For example, some of us would rather learn by listening, discussing, and by taking notes. Others need to see the information and learn better when there are visual representations of the learning. Still others would rather learn by doing. These are the students who say, "Just give me the information and let me do it."

The plasticity of the human brain—the way it continues to change in response to different stimuli—is thought to contribute to the development of preferred learning styles. According to Sprenger (2002), these preferences or strengths may have been brought about through positive experiences: "We use the networks of neurons that solve our problems for us in the easiest and fastest way. As we continue to use those same neurons, the connections become stronger. Therefore if an auditory learner gets positive results from listening and dialoguing, he or she will continue to do so as a preference, and that modality will be strengthened through use." As a matter of fact, there is strong evidence that points to the fact that a so-called slow learner must be retaught in the modality most comfortable for him or her if that student is to be successful (Jensen, 1997).

Schools of the past have relied heavily on lecture as a primary teaching method. Lecture assumes that students learn auditorily, yet through brain research we know that the majority does not learn that way. Only about 20 percent of students learn auditorily; the other 80 percent learn either visually or kinesthetically (Sousa, 2006). While lecture has its place in some courses, it should be used only in short segments—15 minutes or fewer, depending on the age of the student. It is unrealistic to believe that students who are constantly stimulated by the multimedia world will sit for hours each day passively listening to lectures, taking notes, and preparing for a pencil-and-paper exam without dropping out mentally. Life is not a spectator sport; it is an exercise in active involvement, and education should reflect that active involvement.

We are born into this world with a tremendous capacity to learn and with the wiring to make it happen. If you had been born in the early part of the last century, your world would have been based largely on listening, reading, and talking. Radio would have been the primary means of gaining national information and entertainment. Reading books was also a way to enlighten and learn—as well as to entertain. If you were privileged, you might have had access to a piano in your home for playing and listening. Your brain became wired to listen, and thus an educational program based on reading and listening was comfortable for you.

Today's students are a part of a multimedia world from birth. They don't just listen; they participate. They don't just sit; they move. Three-year-olds can perform simple computer skills. Why, then, would we think that today's students would be happy learners sitting and listening all day? They aren't restless to make us crazy; their brains are wired to participate. According to Marc Prensky (2006), by the time students today are 21, they will have played more than 10,000 hours of video games, sent and received 250,000 e-mails and text/instant messages, spent 10,000 hours talking on the phone, watched more than 20,000 hours of television, and been exposed to 500,000 commercials. How could we expect them to be actively involved in a classroom without movement and interaction?

In a study led by Marion Diamond (Diamond, Scheibel, Murphy, & Harvey, 1985), baby rats and mature rats were placed in the same cage with rat toys. This is the environment identified by Diamond as enriched and is the environment in which rats in other studies showed brain growth. In this study, the older rats did not allow the baby rats the opportunity to use the rat toys. As a result, the baby rats did not grow dendrites, though the mature rats continued to do so. Diamond concluded that "it isn't enough for students to be in an enriched environment, they need to help create that environment and be active in it."

In order to better understand how learning takes place, we need to examine the modalities through which the majority of our new learning comes. Figure 2.1 identifies the senses or modalities that bring into our brains new learning and new experiences. Note that overall, the brain filters out about 99 percent of incoming stimuli. The upside to that phenomenon is that if we attended to all of the incoming stimuli, we would be phobic. The downside is that some of the information that we had hoped our students would remember is lost.

Figure 2.1 Learning Through the Senses

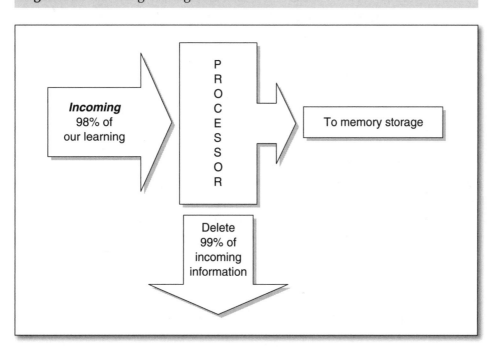

AUDITORY LEARNERS

Auditory learners are those who remember information best when they hear and discuss it. Auditory information is processed and stored in the temporal lobes on the sides of the brain (Jensen, 2006). Auditory students make up about 20 percent of the classroom. They like lecture, adapt well to it, and tend to be successful in our traditional schools. However, in order for the information to have *personal* meaning to auditory learners, it must be discussed or talked through by the learner: Just hearing and taking notes is not enough. In Chapter 1, I discussed the fact that motivation is based in part on the learner's belief that the information has personal meaning. For these learners, that will only occur after they have been given time to talk it through either to themselves or with each other.

Typically, as I've written elsewhere (Tileston 2004b), students who are auditory learners

- like to talk and enjoy activities in which they can talk to their peers or give their opinion,
- encourage people to laugh,
- are good storytellers,
- may show signs of hyperactivity or poor fine-motor coordination,
- usually like listening activities,
- and can memorize easily.

Sprenger (2002) supplies some additional information that can help to identify these students. The auditory learners in your classroom may behave in the following ways:

- They might look out the window while you are talking but be completely aware of what is being said. Such a learner does not need the visual context of looking at the teacher in order to learn.
- They like to talk and discuss. Learning does not have meaning until he or she has had a chance to discuss it either with someone else or with himself or herself. As a matter of fact, an auditory learner may move his or her lips while reading.
- They have difficulty sitting for long periods of time without opportunities for verbalization.

It is important to add that, though these students learn best by hearing, even they grow weary in a straight lecture format. The work of Sousa (2006) and others shows that all of us tend to drop out mentally after 15 or 20 minutes of lecture. In young children, the mental dropout time is significantly less—about 10 minutes. Current indicators are that these numbers may be decreasing slightly for adults and children due to the impact of "instant everything" technology. For example, we once said that we could use a child's age to determine how long he or she could listen at a time: six minutes for a six-year-old. However, indicators point to the fact that this listening span is decreasing as technology has become part of our everyday lives.

Sousa (2006) says that working memory is temporal and deals with information for only a short amount of time before deciding whether or not to discard it. As I stated earlier, the typical time span is about 5 to 10 minutes for preadolescents and 10 to 15 minutes for adolescents. Using this information as a guide, secondary teachers should give information for about 15 minutes and then follow it with activities or discussion to reinforce the learning. Elementary teachers should use four to seven minutes as their guide. Sousa refers to the teaching segments as "prime time." During the first 20 minutes of class, he says, students learn best. New information, information that is of primary importance, should be taught during this time. Figure 2.2 shows how a teacher might use these learning rhythms to enhance student learning.

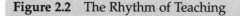

Figure 2.2   The Rhythm of Teaching

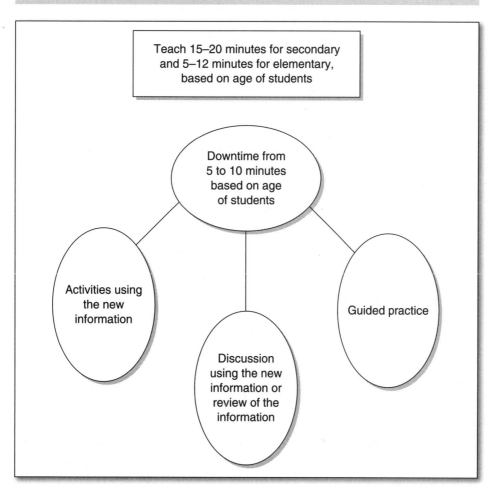

Teaching Auditory Learners

Differentiation does not mean that teachers must teach the same lesson several ways but rather that a variety of techniques should be used. It also means that for students who do not "get it" the first time, a different approach—one more compatible to that student—should be employed the second time. Jensen (1997) says that slow learners will not "get it" until we teach them in the modality most comfortable for them.

Try the following suggestions (Tileston, 2004c) for working with auditory learners:

- Use direct instruction, in which the teacher guides the learning through the application of declarative (what students need to know) and procedural (what students can do with the learning) objectives.
- Employ peer tutoring, in which students help each other practice the learning.
- Plan activities that incorporate music.
- Teach using group discussions, brainstorming, and Socratic seminars.
- Assign specific oral activities.
- Verbalize while learning, including self-talk by the teacher and the learner.
- Use cooperative learning activities that provide for student interaction.

VISUAL LEARNERS

The second type of learning modality is *visual*. Visual information is processed and stored in the occipital lobe at the back of the brain. Visual learners are those who need a mental model that they can see. As I've noted elsewhere (Tileston, 2004c), visual learners are those students who

- have difficulty understanding oral directions,
- may have difficulty remembering names,
- enjoy looking at books or drawing pictures,
- watch the speaker's face,
- like to work puzzles,
- notice small details,
- like for the teacher to use visuals when talking,
- and like to use nonlinguistic organizers.

I am convinced that we could raise math scores immediately all over this country if we could find a way to show kids how math works. Since the majority of learners are visual learners, we need to find ways to show them visually how math works. When I work with audiences, I give them the following problem to solve: if five people shake hands with each other, how many handshakes is that? Now, there is a formula that can be applied to find the answer, and the math people in the audience are quick to work the answer out mathematically. But I like to show the answer visually, because it opens up a new world to people in the audience who need to see how the math works. My visual answer is in Figure 2.3. All that is left is to add up the handshakes: $4 + 3 + 2 + 1 + 0 = 10$ handshakes.

Figure 2.3 A Visual Math Solution

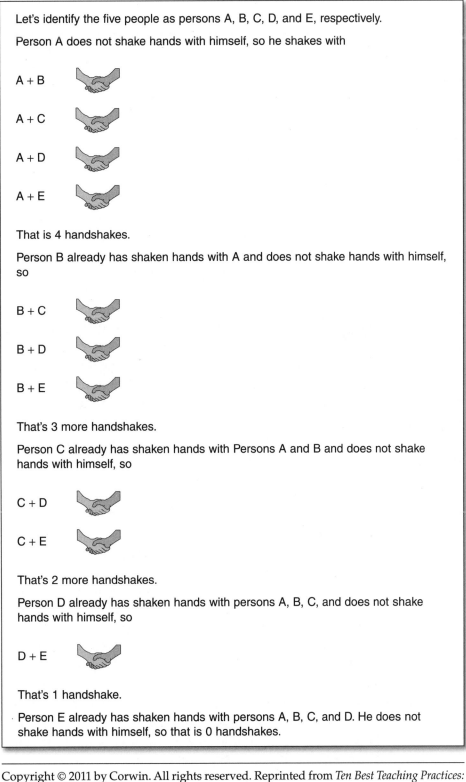

Let's identify the five people as persons A, B, C, D, and E, respectively.

Person A does not shake hands with himself, so he shakes with

A + B

A + C

A + D

A + E

That is 4 handshakes.

Person B already has shaken hands with A and does not shake hands with himself, so

B + C

B + D

B + E

That's 3 more handshakes.

Person C already has shaken hands with Persons A and B and does not shake hands with himself, so

C + D

C + E

That's 2 more handshakes.

Person D already has shaken hands with persons A, B, C, and does not shake hands with himself, so

D + E

That's 1 handshake.

Person E already has shaken hands with persons A, B, C, and D. He does not shake hands with himself, so that is 0 handshakes.

By the way, the formula is

$$(x)(x-1)/2$$

A more complicated version—"One hundred people at the local grocery store shake hands. How many handshakes is that?"—is less threatening once we understand how it works.

Using Nonlinguistic Organizers

One of the most effective tools for visual learners is the nonlinguistic organizer, so called because it relies on structure rather than a lot of words to convey meaning. These organizers help students understand and remember difficult concepts such as sequencing, comparing and contrasting, and classifying. While they are a good teaching strategy for any student, they are important tools for visual students.

The Mid-Continent Regional Education Laboratory (MCREL) looked at studies of the most effective teaching practices for the classroom. They set up a control group to test the studies (meta-analysis) to determine whether current strategies had any effect on student learning and, if so, how much of an effect. While this work is ongoing, the meta-analysis studies on the use of nonlinguistic organizers are significant. They found that when nonlinguistic organizers were taught and used appropriately, students on average gained percentile points. For example, if a class average is at the 50th percentile and nonlinguistic organizers are incorporated into the learning, the class average can be moved to the 79th percentile. That is the difference between failure (50) and success (79) (Marzano, 2001b).

Nonlinguistic organizers can be effectively incorporated into classroom learning to achieve many purposes, including the following:

- *To help students connect or relate new information to prior knowledge.* Because these organizers make abstract ideas more visible, they help students understand and remember concepts that are difficult to visualize otherwise. Young students who have difficulty with abstract concepts can be helped by learning to use a set of visual models that makes the abstract concrete. I believe we can raise the scores of students on standardized tests by giving students concrete models to help them perform difficult skills. By taking the information that they know and placing it in a concrete model, students are able to transfer abstract thoughts to concrete ideas more easily. Figure 2.4 is an example of a mind map depicting a student's prior knowledge of a topic before the learning. As new information is added, the mind map will add spokes to connect the new knowledge.

Figure 2.4   Mind Map Using Different Shapes

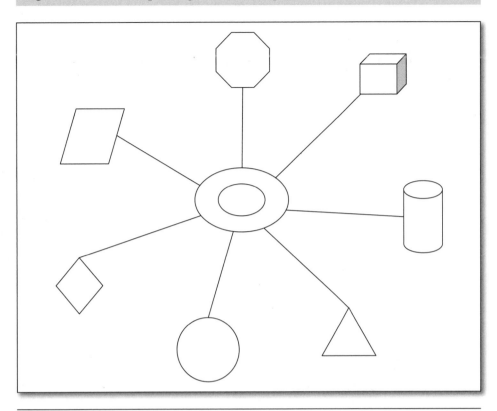

- *To help students create mental models necessary for understanding.* Have you ever read a page in a book and realized at the end of the page that you have no idea what you just read? Perhaps your mind was on something else as your eyes skimmed the page, or maybe the text density was such that it was difficult to make meaning as you read. For struggling students, experiences in the classroom may be much like reading or hearing words that have no meaning. One of the ways that we can help our students make meaning out of the information is by helping them to create mental models of the learning. While there are probably thousands of different organizers on the market today, I have found that they all still fall into general patterns similar to those that Marzano (2001a) describes, such as the following:

  o Descriptive patterns are organizers similar to mind maps that are used to describe or give the critical attributes of something.

  o Sequence patterns are graphic organizers such as might be used for a timeline.

- A process/cause pattern (sometimes called a fishbone) allows the user to determine the causes of something when we already know the outcome. For example, a student might do a fishbone organizer on the causes of World War II.
- Problem/solution patterns provide the problem at the top with possible solutions below the problem.
- A generalization pattern is used when we want to provide information on a principle. Figure 2.5 is an example of this pattern. We are examining the issue of motivation to learn in the example provided.

- *To help students use information.* Nonlinguistic organizers can be used at any time during the learning process, but they are critical in the lesson phase in which the teacher wants the students to use the information in some way. This is a time for clarifying ideas for both the student and the teacher—prior to assessment. This is a great way to teach the real-world application. Ask students to demonstrate understanding by showing a way that the new learning is used in the real world.

Figure 2.5   Generalization Pattern

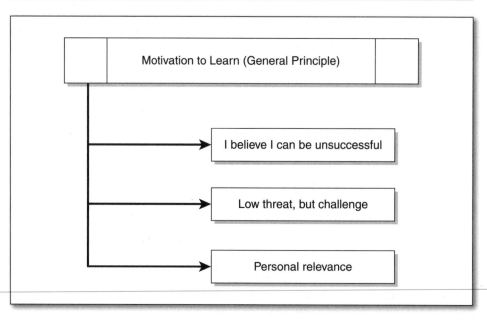

- *To introduce a difficult or abstract concept.* The old adage that a picture is worth a thousand words is absolutely true. Many students have difficulty with logic problems: A matrix is a visual tool that helps make this complex skill more manageable.
- *To assess the learning.* Instead of having students list items from the learning, give them a choice to mind map it. For example, you could give this instruction: "Mind map the key points we discussed in science class today."
- *As part of an individual or group project.* Examples might be mind maps, flow charts, or attribute webs. When these tools are used at the application level or above, they can be important products in student projects.
- *To demonstrate creativity.* Visual students, once they have been exposed to visual models, have little trouble adding creative and elaborative touches to their models.
- *To depict relationships between facts and concepts.* Cause-and-effect, fishbone, and Venn diagrams are examples of mental maps that depict relationships.
- *To generate and organize ideas for writing.* Mind maps and stratification maps are great tools to help students organize their thoughts before writing.
- *To relate new information to prior knowledge.* For a new unit, tap into students' prior knowledge and apply those experiences to the new knowledge they are about to gain. For example, prior to a unit on explorers, ask students if they have ever set a goal and then had difficulty achieving that goal. Have students mind map how they overcame the constraints.
- *To store and retrieve information.* One of my favorite visuals takes vocabulary words—including those in other languages—and draws icons to symbolize the meaning of the words. Students who are visual will see the icons as they retrieve the information from their brains.
- *To assess student thinking and learning.* Ask students to mindmap the key information in a chapter or lesson.
- *To depict relationships between facts and concepts.* Use a matrix to help students make connections from general concepts to determining what are facts and what are not.

Teaching Visual Learners

Some additional ideas for working with visual learners include the following:

- Use visuals when teaching. Remember, these students need to "see" the learning for it to make sense.

- Directly teach students to use visual organizers and provide enough practice so that the process is automatic to the student.
- Show students the patterns in the learning. Remember, the brain likes patterns, and it is the connections that create these patterns that help raise our level of understanding.

Anytime we can help visual learners see the information with visuals, we help them process more efficiently, and we provide a connector so that they can retrieve the information more efficiently from long-term memory. Have you ever had a student say to you on test day, "I know I know the answer; I just can't think of it!" The truth is that it is probably stored in long-term memory, but the student lacks a connector or the language skills (for English language learners) to be able to retrieve it. The semantic memory system that stores factual information is the least reliable of the memory systems and needs a connector to help students retrieve the information. Otherwise, it is much like visiting your local bookstore and finding it has shelved books in random order, and you must search the whole store in hopes of finding the book you need.

KINESTHETIC LEARNERS

The third learning modality is *kinesthetic*. Kinesthetic information is stored at the top of the brain in the motor cortex until permanently learned, and then it is stored in the cerebellum, the area below the occipital lobe (Jensen, 1998). Kinesthetic learners learn best through movement and touching. In the previous handshake exercise (Figure 2.3), kinesthetic learners would solve the problem by physically shaking hands with four other people and counting the handshakes.

As I've written elsewhere (Tileston 2004c), kinesthetic learners may

- need the opportunity to be mobile;
- want to feel, smell, and taste everything;
- want to touch their neighbor as well;
- usually have good motor skills and may be athletic;
- like to take things apart to see how they work;
- may appear immature for their age group;
- and may be hyperactive learners.

Teaching Kinesthetic Learners

Kinesthetic learners, according to Sprenger (2002), are characterized by the following:

- Need hands-on activities. The learning will not have meaning until they have an opportunity to do something with it.

- Respond to physical closeness and physical rewards, such as a pat on the back.
- May become discipline problems in a traditional setting unless they are given the opportunity for movement.
- May slump down in their seats (the comfort of the room is important to them) or may wiggle a great deal in traditional classrooms.

Provide opportunities for your class to go outside, go on field trips, or role-play. In addition, and whenever possible, provide opportunities for them to move around in the classroom, to change groups, or just to stand. The old adage that we think better on our feet is absolutely true. When we stand, we increase the flow of fluids to the brain, and we do learn better. Take advantage of that in the classroom by having students stand to give answers or to discuss with each other.

Providing opportunities for movement in the classroom can make a tremendous difference in the behavior and learning for these students. Try the following suggestions (Tileston, 2004c) for meeting the needs of these students:

- Use a hands-on approach to learning.
- Provide opportunities to move.
- Use simulations when appropriate.
- Bring in music, art, and manipulatives.
- Break up a lecture so that it is in manageable chunks (a good rule is to talk to a student only for the number of minutes equal to his or her age—for a 10-year-old, 10 minutes).
- Use discovery learning when appropriate.
- Use such techniques as discussion groups or cooperative learning so that these students have an opportunity to move about and talk with their peers.

MEASURING SUCCESS

Figure 2.6 shows common indicators of success for teaching effectively to reach all students, regardless of whether they are auditory, visual, or kinesthetic learners.

Figure 2.6 Indicators of a Classroom in Which a Variety of Teaching Strategies Are Used to Address Different Learning Styles

Evaluation Tool	Indicators of Success
Teaching time	Follows the rhythm of the brain, with 15 or fewer minutes of instruction followed by 5–10 minutes, for secondary students, in which the students do something with the learning or, for elementary students, instruction in approximately 10-minute segments followed by opportunities to work with the new learning
Lesson plans	Indicate opportunities for students to stand and move, to go on field trips, and to explore the environment
Lesson plans	Indicate a variety of visual tools are used
Student projects	Indicate choices that include visual, kinesthetic, and auditory learning
Teaching practices	All reteaching is done in the preferred modality of the learner.

CONCLUSION

Although we all record information using all three modalities, most of us have a preference for one over the other two. Sousa (2006) says teachers need to understand that students with different sensory preferences will behave differently during learning and that teachers tend to teach the way they learn. That explains, in part, why so many students have trouble learning from one teacher but may learn easily from another. Behavior interpreted to mean that the student was not interested in the learning or did not want to learn may, in fact, have only been an indication of inappropriate teaching techniques or a classroom where only one modality was valued. The classroom that is enriched with teaching techniques from all three modalities will be a place where quality learning is possible.

3

Helping Students Make Connections From Prior Knowledge

Being student-centered also means connecting learning to students' lives, using the student's own culture, strengths (intelligences), interests, goals, and dreams as the beginning point for learning.

—Bonnie Benard (2003)

Schools today are making strides as never before to help students connect to content. Our classrooms look very different from those even five years ago as we have a growing number of students from minority cultures and as the dominant culture of the classroom changes rapidly. The U.S. Census Bureau (2006) says that by the year 2012, the dominant race in the classroom will be Hispanic with African Americans second and those of Anglo-Saxon European descent third. If we are to teach the children of our classrooms, rather than the children of past classrooms, we must take into account the background knowledge that they bring to the classroom.

We know that when we teach new information the brain will make sense of it sooner if there is a prior connection with which to create a pattern.

Indeed, the human brain seems to be wired to seek connections. Anytime we are given new information, there is an effort within the structure of the brain to attach that new information to knowledge or experiences already in place. Thus, it makes sense that the more we can help students make connections between what they already know and the new knowledge, the more we are apt to provide positive learning experiences.

Marzano (2007) refers to teaching essential learning goals as critical–input experiences that require a step-by-step process if students are going to understand and be able to use the new learning. For example, suppose a teacher is introducing a new unit on fractions. One of the goals of the learning is to help students understand the concept of fractional parts. Another goal is to help students use their background knowledge of everyday things that are composed of fractional parts so that they can create mental models of the learning.

What can this teacher do to help students tap into what they already know about fractions to help them create the mental models necessary for learning and remembering? Some of the ways that teachers might do this include these suggestions (based on the model by Marzano, 2007).

- Ask questions or provide a graphic organizer such as a KWL to find out what students already know about fractional parts. For this lesson, the teacher might ask, "How many of you eat pizza?" and "Did you know that when you buy a pizza, it is cut into fractional parts?"
- Link the new learning to prior learning in the classroom. "We have been studying whole numbers so far this year, but what can we do if we are dividing and do not get a whole number?
- Ask preview questions to help the students think about the new learning in advance. For the lesson on fractions, the teacher might ask the following:
  o When you buy a slice of pizza is it always the same size?
  o How many slices of pizza make up a whole pizza?
  o If I pay $2 for a slice of pizza and it is $1/8^{th}$ of a whole pizza, but the next day I pay $2 and it is $1/16^{th}$ of a whole pizza, have I been cheated?

- The teacher might provide a brief summary of the new learning either in writing or orally.
- Ask students to skim the textbook by looking at the main headings or subheadings or even pictures and graphics to see if they can determine what the reading will be about. Students do this all the time with technology. They will look at the headings and pictures usually before reading the text. Do you know a child who actually reads all the directions to a new video game before playing? What do they do? They skim the pictures, the main points, and then they play.

- The teacher might prepare notes for the students that help them to follow the lesson and to know the key ideas. The notes might look like a simple outline, much as I have given you on tapping into prior learning. I often do this with my graduate students early in the semester to demonstrate to them how to take good notes. As they become adept at it, I withdraw the teacher-made outline.

Caution Zone

Remember that if you are creating an experience or questions prior to the new learning to help your students connect prior knowledge and experiences to the new knowledge, that the questions and experiences must be relevant to the culture of the students. For example, a friend of mine recently told me of an experience some of the Hispanic students in her school encountered. She lives in a state where Hispanic students from Mexico are new to the area, and most educators have not worked with this culture before and do not know a great deal about the culture itself. Students were asked to discuss preparing for summer camp in advance of the new learning. These students had not experienced summer camp and in fact did not understand the concept: for people to pay to go to a camp in the summer seemed ridiculous to these students from poverty.

Sousa (2006) refers to the brain's process of making connections between old and new learning as *transfer*. The strength of this process is dependent on two factors. First, the effect of the past learning on the new learning and, second, the degree to which the new learning will be useful in the future. When new information is introduced to working memory, a search is conducted in long-term memory for past learning that connects to the new learning. When those connections are made successfully, greater achievement is possible. Sousa (2006) refers to this as *positive transfer*. Negative transfer occurs when past learning interferes with new learning. Sousa uses the example of learning to drive a standard shift car after driving only an automatic shift car in the past. The skill of leaving the left foot on the floor of the car for driving an automatic shift car can be a hindrance if transferred to the standard shift car where the left foot must be moved onto the clutch for shifting.

TAPPING INTO PRIOR KNOWLEDGE

In today's diverse classrooms, students come to us with a wide variety of experiences and, depending on the makeup of the classroom, those experiences may vary greatly. How, then, do we use past experiences or background knowledge of our students to help them create connections to the new learning?

First, we must examine our own background knowledge about our students. Do you know what kinds of learning experiences your students

It is not a matter of knowing every culture but of knowing the students in your classroom.

bring to the classroom, especially if the children in your classroom do not look like you? What are the cultural differences of your students? All of us are a part of several cultures, and those cultures affect our experiences and the way that we view all things in the world. We have cultural differences informed by race, religion, first and subsequent languages, geographical locale, and social affiliations, among other factors. Just taking a cultural awareness class—many of which are not much more than Tacos on Tuesday—is not going to be of much help to you in determining how these factors have influenced the past experiences of your students and how they affect learning.

Here are some ways that you can find out about the students you teach:

Learn about the neighborhoods in which your students live. Look at them in terms of the languages spoken, the prevalent occupations, the kinds of holidays celebrated, and the opportunities for enriched educational experiences available to the students there. To the extent possible tie the new learning to the experiences that your students bring to the classroom. The Mid-Continent Regional Educational Lab (McREL) provides a sample lesson on "Explorers Through Time" (2002). In this lesson, students begin the unit by discussing a time when they had something that they wanted but were hindered by things they could control (constraints) and things they could not control (limiting conditions). Through a graphic organizer, students discuss what they did to overcome both the limiting conditions and the constraints and what the final result was for them. The teacher was using past experiences to help students understand that all people who achieve have constraints that they must overcome. Marie Curie, for example, was a woman scientist at a time when it was not appropriate for women to be scientists. What a great way to begin a unit on explorers! Not only do students tie what their experiences have been to the experiences of famous explorers, but they learn that all of us have conditions that we can control and some we cannot and that the key to success is finding ways to overcome both. Students from poverty often believe that they have no locus of control and that they just have bad luck (see http://www.mcrel .org/compendium/activityDetail.asp?activityID=181).

Provide materials and visuals that reflect the culture of the classroom. What does your room look like in terms of the students that you teach? In the elementary classroom, make sure that you have reading materials that reflect and appeal to your students' various cultures. The pictures and posters on the walls and the pictures that you use in your lessons should reflect the ethnicities of the classroom. Take suggestions from your students about how to decorate the room and what music to use.

Every neighborhood has "movers and shakers" so find out who they are. Who are the parents and grandparents that everyone listens to? Is there a ministerial alliance that works in the community and has influence with students and caregivers?

Use technology to communicate with parents (and students). Even in very poor neighborhoods we have found that parents and other care-givers tell us they can use technology at work to check messages and to look at school websites. We sometimes assume parents don't come to the school because of lack of concern when, in fact, parents care very much. Trying to feed a family and pay bills in a down economy takes away our energy and our ability to visit school at the hours specified by the school for conferences. Be creative and find alternative ways to communicate with parents; this will give you a window into the world of your students and help you to build better connections to the learning.

BUILDING PRIOR KNOWLEDGE IN THE CLASSROOM

What if there are no prior experiences and knowledge on the subject to be taught? We have said that the brain is a seeker of connections. We have all had the experience of being in a room where something is being discussed about which we have no knowledge. There is confusion and frustration while we work to find a connection or hook for the new information. For some students, this is a daily occurrence. What this means in the classroom is that we cannot assume that students come to us with the structures already in place to learn new material. We must first establish what they know and understand and, where there are no previous connections, supply them for the student.

In meta-analysis studies conducted through MCREL, building connections *prior* to the learning had a high effect size on student learning. Marzano (1998) calls this strategy "direct schema activation." In the studies conducted, the average achievement score was raised by 27 percentile points representing an effect size of 0.75. This means that, in a classroom in which the average student is at the 50th percentile range, the class average can be moved above the 70th percentile range just by correctly employing this technique in the teaching process.

Let's look at some of the ways that we can build prior knowledge in the classroom during a lesson.

- Use advance organizers to help students build knowledge throughout the unit. We discussed earlier that we might give our students an outline for taking notes and following an oral lesson. Advance organizers help students to make sense of the new learning by providing a structure and a pattern for learning. Figure 3.1 is an example of an advance organizer for a lesson in which students will be studying vocabulary. This organizer contains the information that students will need to know about the vocabulary.

Figure 3.1 Word Chart

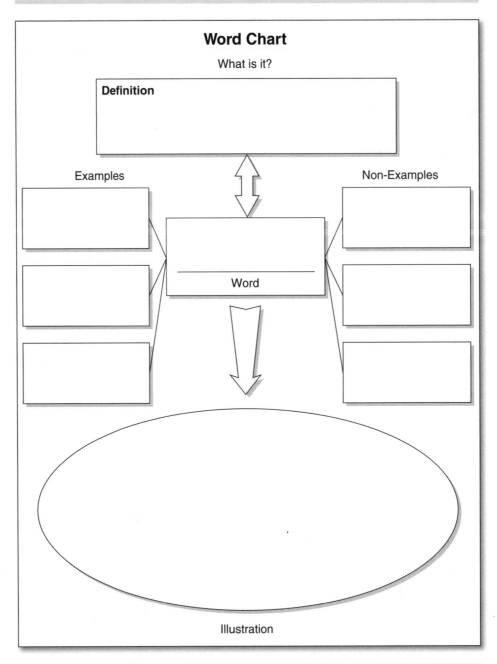

Figure 3.1 Word Chart

- Use cues and/or questions to help students make connections between what they know and what they are learning. According to Marzano, Norford, Paynter, Pickering, and Gaddy (2001), "Cues are explicit reminders or hints about what students are about to experience" (p. 267). For example, a second-grade teacher about to begin a unit on shapes might tell students that they are going to be studying shapes and that they will discover there are shapes all over the room and that some are behind, in front of, below, beside, and above other things. Questions perform the same kind of task. An example of a question that a teacher might ask prior to a lesson on shapes is, "What shape is the globe on my desk?" The KNLH chart provided in Figure 3.2 (see page 44) is also an excellent way to find out what students already know.

- Use visual imagery and discussion to create prior experience where there is none. For example, for a unit on immigration my students might not have had enough experience to understand why people risk their lives to immigrate. I might want to show a video clip of people fleeing with only the clothes on their backs and risking danger to go to another place. I might ask my students what would cause people to leave a place they have called home and go to a new place where they virtually have to start over, learn a new language, and perhaps even face prejudicial treatment.

Sousa (2006) identifies four factors originally identified by Madeline Hunter that influence the rate and degree of retrieval. They include *association/context*, *similarity*, *critical attributes*, and *degree of original learning*. In the following sections, let's look at the four factors and how classroom teachers might use those factors to help students make connections in the classroom.

Association/Context

Sousa defines *association* as events, actions, or feelings that are learned together so that the recall of one prompts the recall of the other. In my books *Strategies for Teaching Differently* (Walker, 1998) and *Strategies for Active Learning* (Tileston, 2006), I refer to this part of the lesson as *personal connection*, because it is the process of providing a hook or connection that makes the learning personal. Personal or association connection is based on the association of past experience, past knowledge, or, in the event that there are no past experiences, on the associations that we create. It is the process of going from the known to the unknown.

This is probably the most common way that teachers help students bridge the new-learning gap. We want to find some experience or information that the student already has in long-term memory to which we can connect the new information. This is why teachers often refer back to previous lessons if the information to be studied requires the prerequisite of the information from the previous lesson. When there is no previous lesson from which to draw, we can create the hook with personal experiences the students may have had. If we can draw from personal experiences, especially those with emotional ties, we have a greater chance of making the new information relevant to the learner. The previous example on explorers is a good example of how we can hook students into the learning by using their own problems that they encounter in trying to reach goals. By looking at how famous explorers overcame great obstacles, students can gain new ways to solve their own problems. In working with children from poverty, we want to build resiliency. Bonnie Benard says that resiliency is the ability to be successful in spite of our circumstances (Benard, 2003).

As mentioned in Chapter 1, the brain ties itself to strong emotions. The amygdala, found in the forebrain, is responsible for encoding emotional messages and bonding them to the learning for long-term storage. Emotion is so strong in the brain that it takes priority over everything else. We are therefore more likely to remember something when we have an emotional tie to it. I often ask audiences to think back to the youngest age they can remember. The events they remember are usually either very happy or traumatic. Both are strong emotional ties. Emotions can also have a negative effect on making connections. Students who have always experienced problems with math will come to math class with negative transfer even before the lessons begin. We can change that emotional state by providing opportunities for success—not just once, but over time. We do this by providing students with scaffolding to help them to fill the gaps in learning and to better understand how the learning works. For example, in mathematics, a student may dread class because he does not understand how to solve the given problems. As a teacher, I might find out how he prefers to learn—does he need visuals, or does he need manipulatives to help him understand how the math works? Because most students today are visual and kinesthetic (due in part to the bombardment of technology on the brain since birth), just memorizing formulas is not enough; they need to see how the math works. Providing success by watering down the material is the least effective way to change the learning state and may actually cause the student to lose ground.

When drawing on past experiences to which students may have emotional ties to introduce new information, the following examples might be used. Whisler and Williams (1990) give this example: In elementary school, prior to reading *Earrings* by Judith Viorst, ask, "Have you ever wanted to do something that your parents said you could not because you weren't old enough?" In middle school, prior to a lesson on the Boston Tea Party, ask, "Have you ever encountered a rule that you felt was unfair to you in some way? Did you try to talk to someone about it? Did they listen?"

Personal or association connection is the piece that gives ownership to the learning process. Prior to a lesson on estimation, ask, "Have you ever seen those contests where you must guess how many jelly beans are in a jar?" By giving the problem personal application, we create ownership. All of us are more interested in things to which we feel personal attachment: "What kind of strategy would you use to win the contest?" Prediction is another way we help create ownership to the learning by using students' natural curiosity to hook them into the learning. This is the marketing to which I referred earlier. We want to know about tomorrow's weather so we can plan accordingly, so we wait diligently during the news. Just before the commercial break, the newscaster says, "Big changes coming in the weather; stay tuned after our commercial break for the details." They have us hooked so we will stay around for the details. This is a great technique to hook kids into reading and learning material that otherwise might not seem exciting. Fitzgerald (1996) gives these examples of using prediction to hook kids into the learning:

> A science teacher is introducing a unit on electro-magnetic radiation so he holds an electric razor up to an electro-magnetic radiation meter to set off the warning light. (An indication of radiation above the recommended level for human tissue.) A speech teacher shows clips from the Kennedy-Nixon debate and asks what skills or lack thereof will influence the outcome.

Elementary teachers often use this technique by showing pictures or giving information prior to reading a story to pique the kids' interest. A secondary teacher says, "In *Romeo and Juliet* there is going to be a major fight between two gangs tonight. What do you think will happen?" Sousa (2006) says that these hooks or connections should be given to students a day, even a week, before the learning to give them thinking time to get interested in the subject.

Personal or association connection is the link between previous knowledge and new knowledge, as in this lesson: "Last week, we talked about slope and how it is used in the real world to figure the dimensions of wheelchair ramps. Today, we are going to measure wheelchair ramps around the building. Before we do that, let's review what the law says about the dimensions of these ramps and how we determine slope." Not only are we linking knowledge, but we have also heightened the need to know with the fact that the students are going to do something with the information.

Figure 3.2 is an association tool that I use to help students make connections between old learning and experiences to the new learning. The *K* represents the old "knowledge, skills, and experiences" that students have with the subject. The *N* represents information that students will "need to know" about the topic. This is another way of setting personal goals for the learning. The *L* represents "learned information" that is completed after studying the topic. The importance of this metacognitive activity is to help students synthesize what they have learned. Jensen (1998) says that we do not know something until we are convinced that we know it. Until then, it is just meaningless information. Have you ever been to an all-day conference in which you were bombarded with a great deal of new information that you were sure you would remember and use only to find when you got back to your school that it was a jumble? The *H* represents "how you learned the information." The "how" of the process is important because it helps bridge the gap between the borrowed opinions of others to the personalized and warranted opinions discovered by the learner.

Figure 3.2 KNLH (Know/Need to Know/Learned/How Learned) Chart

Know	Need to Know	Learned	How Learned

Categories 1.

2.

3.

4.

5.

Before introducing a new unit, I ask my students to brainstorm ideas or information that they already know about the new subject. Figure 3.3 is a graphic organizer that I use to help students put the information into an organized structure to help them see the connections.

Those thoughts and information gleaned from the brainstorming session are written in the center circle of the organizer. For example, for our unit on world hunger, I ask them to list everything they already know about world hunger in the inner circle of Figure 3.3. Then, I ask them to look at the information that they have listed and to place any information that would be related to transportation in the Category 1 circle, anything that would be related to politics in the Category 2 circle, anything that would be related to medical conditions in the Category 3 circle, and so on. By asking students not only to recall information but also to put it into categories, I am providing word associations early in the learning to help them retrieve information when they need it. This exercise also provides the teacher with important

Figure 3.3   Using Categories to Describe Words

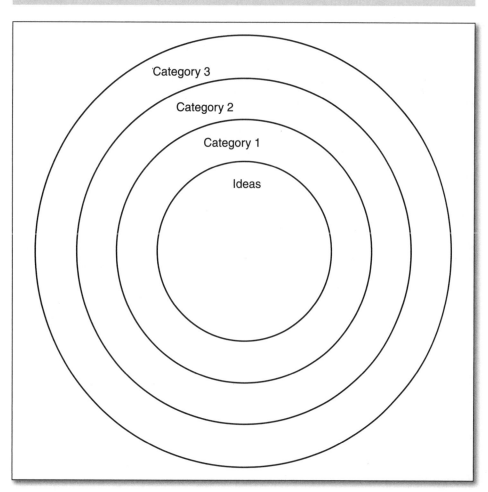

information: what do students already know about this subject that doesn't need to be retaught, and what misinformation do they have that needs to be corrected up front before they place it in long-term memory?

A word of caution on any technique used to introduce a lesson: be sure that incorrect information is corrected immediately so that it does not become a part of long-term memory. We tend to remember those things that are discussed in the first 20 minutes of class, so it is critical that we make the most of that time in getting important facts on the table correctly.

After the students have made their lists and we have made a class master list from their information, I give them a lead-in or emotional hook to create interest. I might say, "In this country, we produce enough food each year for every man, woman, and child in the world to have 2,500 calories each day, so why do we have world hunger?" By giving them an interesting tidbit of information about world hunger—that it is not a matter of food production, which most of them thought—I hook them into the learning. Then, I lead them to ask questions. This approach is not unlike the evening news programs that give us a small amount of information just before a commercial break to keep us watching. I ask, "So, what would you like to know about world hunger?" From the information that they provide, I make a "want to know" list. During the unit on world hunger, we will refer back to this list often so that students can see that their questions and concerns are being answered. By doing this, I am giving them a *personal connection* or association to the learning.

Association or personal connection can also be the bridge between disciplines. There are many natural links between disciplines, and we need to point these out to students. We cannot assume that they will naturally get the relationship between the study of World War II in history and the study of the John Hersey's novel *Hiroshima* in English class. In our restructured high school, we had a wedding to marry math to science and English to history. Teachers worked across disciplines to realign the curriculum so that those natural connections could take place at the same time. We did not change *what* we taught, just *when* we taught it. As we became more cognizant of what our colleagues were teaching, the benefits were transferred to our students. Departments made joint assignments so that, instead of several fragmented projects, the projects moved across disciplines. Because students were working on fewer individual projects, they could present more complex, in-depth projects. In elementary school, we have a natural vehicle for doing this, since the schedule allows the same teacher to teach across disciplines. As schools become more advanced in this technique and as student e-mail is introduced into classrooms, students will have opportunities to create projects that not only go across disciplines but across grade levels as well.

Similarity

Sousa defines *similarity* as the process of transfer "generated by the similarity of the situation in which something is being learned and the situation to which that learning may transfer" (2006, p.142). Thus, behavior in one environment tends to transfer to other environments that are similar.

He uses the example of pilots who are trained in simulators and then transfer that experience to the actual plane.

In my book *Strategies for Active Learning* (Tileston, 2006), I use similarity when students do not have exact prior knowledge or experience to connect to the new learning. In this instance, I relate the new information to something similar that they already understand personally.

Critical Attributes

Sousa identifies *critical attributes* as "characteristics that make one idea unique from all others" (2006, p.144). *Unique* is the key word here, since it is important that students identify how things are different so that retrieval will be easier. Sousa says that long-term memory files new information into a network with similar information, but, when it retrieves it, memory looks for differences so that the right piece of information is retrieved. He uses the example that we recognize our best friend not by the attributes that make him or her like everyone else, but by features that make him or her unique. We have all had the experience of looking for someone in a crowd. For a moment, everyone looks alike; they all have faces, bodies, and hair. The way we find the person we are seeking is in looking for features unique to that person, such as black hair, tall body, and sharp chin.

Since the brain already has stored patterns and structures from previous learning and experiences, teachers build on those patterns for similar information that is new. This technique makes use of the brain's search for patterns for understanding. Patterns might be categories, such as those given in the example on immigration, or rhymes and letter games, such as those in mnemonic devices. Graphic models are great tools to help visual students create attributes. Use mind maps or organization tables with key concepts to help students form patterns for the new learning. Since about 85 percent of the learners in a classroom learn either visually or kinesthetically (Jensen, 1998), it is important to include visual models to help connect the learning. I want to note here that since Jensen's work in 1998, we have had a huge increase in the amount of technology used daily by students, and this use of technology has probably increased the percentage of students who are visual or visual/kinesthetic learners. After all, with technology we "see the information first," then read about it, and finally interact with it.

Degree of Original Learning

Sousa (2006) says that when the original learning was well learned and accurate, new learning will be more powerful. This factor is a great argument for teaching a concept for mastery, not just to cover the subject. Many teachers are frustrated by the amount of material that is required by state, national, or local policies without regard to whether the students actually learn it. We can only hope that as brain research is understood, schools will take another look at not only how information is taught, but also at the time frame in which it is taught.

We need to move from a philosophy of covering material to understanding and being able to use information.

MEASURING SUCCESS

Figure 3.4 shows the characteristics of a classroom that indicate the successful use of strategies to help students create connections between prior knowledge and prior classroom learning to new learning.

Figure 3.4   Indicators of a Classroom in Which Curriculum Facilitates Transfer From Prior Learning

Assessment Tools	Indicators of Success
Lesson plans	Students are provided opportunities to create connections to the new learning prior to the beginning of new lessons or units.
	Where prior knowledge and experience do not exist, the teacher provides that information before going to the new material.

CONCLUSION

Never, in the history of education, has the use of prior information been so critical. Why? Because we are teaching students from more varied backgrounds than ever before. The teachers of our parents and for most of us could teach us based on their background knowledge and be close to the background knowledge of their students. More and more, the reverse is true. We must first know our students so that we know how to help them create connections between new and old learning. Next, we must know when to create the background knowledge when it is lacking. Meaning making is dependent on being able to use what we know and connect it effectively to the unknown; otherwise there may be chaos. The number of students from poverty being placed into special education has grown exponentially in the last decade while the number of students in public schools has been declining. We must ask ourselves what we are doing in the classroom to help these students make meaning out of content that may be in a different language than their own and that may not make sense. For example, a student from one of the Hispanic countries may not have heard of George Washington or of the Westward Movement. More and more we must create the background knowledge for our students and find ways to better utilize the background knowledge with which they come.

Eric Jensen (2003) says that the brain thrives on meaning, not random information. We should not assume that students come to us with the necessary structures in place to make the connections to new information and across disciplines. We must first find out what they know, what misinformation they have about the subject, and, where no structures exist, create structures for the new information. When we do this, we help students "get it" from the very beginning. Although it takes some class time to do this, it may very well save time in the long run because reteaching will not be needed to the degree that it would be without it.

4

Teaching for Long-Term Memory

The process of comprehension within the cognitive system is responsible for translating knowledge into a form appropriate for storage in permanent memory.

—Robert Marzano (2001a)

A decade ago, brain researchers believed that we had two basic memories—short-term and long-term memories. More recent research has indicated that our short-term or temporary memory actually functions on two levels. According to Sousa (2005), "Neuroscientists now believe that we have two temporary memories that perform different tasks. It is a way of explaining how the brain deals briefly with some data but can continue to process other data for extended periods of time. For now, short-term memory is used by cognitive neuroscientists to include the two stages of temporary memory: immediate memory and working memory" (p. 46).

Immediate memory: Once new information has entered the brain it is held in immediate memory for a matter of seconds while we decide either consciously or subconsciously whether the information is important or whether we need to toss it out. Our students often perceive that the new learning has no relevance to them or to their goals and may simply toss out the information without sending it to be processed, discussed, or added on to. We can help prevent this with the way in which we present the new information.

Working memory: If the brain has determined that the new information is important, it moves to working memory where it may stay for minutes or even days while it is mulled over and often discussed. At this point, the information has our attention. Sousa (2006) says that preschool students deal with only two items of information at once, whereas preadolescents deal with three to seven items, with the average being five. From adolescence through adulthood, seven to nine chunks are handled at one time, with seven being the average. Jensen (2003) uses a similar guide. He says that infants hold about one item of information in working memory at a time, with the number increasing by one every other year of life to adolescence, where seven to nine items are held in working memory.

Long-term memory: In order to understand long-term memory—where information is sent once it has been processed by working memory—we must look at the brain's storage system. There are a number of memory pathways in the brain, possibly many more than we have yet discovered. Some researchers say that there are five; others say that there are only three. Quite a few different theoretical models have been developed by neuroscientists, but all agree that there are temporary storage systems within working memory and that it's most likely that verbal and visual information travel along separate neural pathways. Corbin (2008) defines long-term memories as the electro-chemical connections or pathways created when we learn something. Those connections are reinforced each time we recall a memory. Our memory pathways are the places in the brain that store those memories and appear to fall into the categories of explicit memory or declarative memory and implicit memory or procedural memory. Declarative memory involves factual information while procedural memory involves processes, skills, and routines. Figure 4.1 is a graphic model of the two types of memory and the pathways—semantic, episodic, sensory, and reflective—that are guided by them.

Figure 4.1   Storage Systems of the Brain

Declarative		Procedural	
Semantic	Episodic	Sensory	Reflective
words	location	skills	conditioned response
symbols	events	processes	emotional response
abstract information	contextual	routines	reflexes
new references			

SEMANTIC MEMORY

Semantic memory holds the information that was learned from words, symbols, and abstractions. This new information enters through the brain stem and passes through the thalamus to the hippocampus, where a search is conducted for stored facts and experiences with which to connect the new learning. If a connection is made, the information will go to working memory (Jensen, 2003). Semantic memory goes to the prefrontal cortex where it is rehearsed and where processing takes place. Semantic memory either has to be rehearsed a sufficient number of times for the learner to remember it, or it has to have a hook or attachment so that the learner can retrieve it from its memory pathway. Neuroscientists refer to two types of rehearsal: rote rehearsal that includes memorization and elaborative rehearsal that includes rehearsal over time. Rote rehearsal is effective when the answer is always the same, such as when learning multiplication tables. Elaborative rehearsal is the most effective method when students are dealing with all other forms of information. The semantic memory system requires that students have good use of language if they are going to store and retrieve information there.

English language learners will especially have difficulty with this retrieval system since it requires that they have good vocabulary skills to retrieve the information stored there. In my book, *Teaching Strategies that Prepare Students for High-Stakes Tests* (Tileston & Darling, 2008a), I discuss the fact that most high-stakes tests are based on the vocabulary of the standards. As a matter of fact, 95 percent of the mastery of a high-stakes test depends on your ability to understand the vocabulary in the standards. Since vocabulary is usually stored in the semantic memory system of the brain, it should be no surprise that the lowest test scores in the nation are among English language learners. Find ways to add context to the vocabulary so that English language learners will store this information in another area of the brain. An easy way to do this is to have students draw a graphic to help them remember the vocabulary definition. By doing this, you provide a hook for retrieval.

Semantic memory is the most difficult to retrieve from long-term storage. Facts, dates, and vocabulary are difficult to memorize without sufficient time, repetition, and hooks to help the learner remember the stored information. Corbin (2008) says that information that would typically be stored in the semantic memory system is more likely to be recalled when it is embedded within the episodic memory system or the memory systems associated with procedural memory since they are much more reliable and brain friendly. As a matter of fact, the brain does not seem to do well with isolated facts since they do not follow a pattern.

Two hooks boost the process. The first hook for semantic memory is relevance or meaning. The question becomes, "What does this have to do with the world in which I live?" We have all had

Two hooks or attachments are important in ensuring that the brain stores the information in long-term memory: relevance and patterns.

students who ask, "When are we ever going to use this?" Students ask not to drive us crazy but because they really need to know in order to make the learning meaningful. Several years ago, I attended one of William Glasser's workshops. Glasser said that he could teach anyone anything as long as he could make it relevant. After all, he said, very young children learn one of the hardest things to learn—a language—and no one stands in front of them with flash cards (Glasser, 1994). They learn it because it is relevant to their world. If we can give the information relevance in the classroom, there is a good chance that it will be remembered. Keefe (1997) says we can create meaning by modeling, by giving examples from experience, and through artificial meaning, such as mnemonic devices.

The second hook for semantic memory is patterns created by prior knowledge or experience. Sousa (2005) calls this "making sense" of the information. Is there already a pattern in place into which the new information can fit? Do I have prior knowledge or prior experience with which to hook onto the new information? Students will be able to learn and remember statistics more easily if they have a prior knowledge of algebra. Jensen (1995) cites the work of Renate Nummela Caine, who concludes, "The ability to make meaningful sense out of countless bits of data is critical to understanding and motivation." Jensen suggests that, prior to the learning, we create a global overview, give oral previews, or post mind maps to help form the patterns for the instruction. During the learning, we should allow students to discuss the topic and to create models, mind maps, or pictures. After finishing a topic, we should give the learners the opportunity to evaluate it, discuss relevance, or demonstrate patterning with models, plays, or teachings. For example, Pat Jacoby (1991) introduces a unit on immigration by asking students what would cause them to leave this country. Next, she asks what would have to happen in this country politically for them to leave. Economically? In the religious arena? By doing that, she provides a hook or pattern for the learning that is about to take place. When students get around to the economic, religious, and political reasons why people emigrate, they have prior learning to create a hook for the new learning. During the lesson, provide opportunities for students to use the information in such visuals as mind maps or through written diagrams. Jensen (1998) says that the semantic memory pathway requires repetition of the learning and needs to be stimulated by associations, comparisons, and similarities. The immigration example makes use of associations in a concrete way.

Of the two hooks, relevance and patterns, Sousa (2005) says the most important is relevance. He goes on to say that most classrooms spend the majority of lesson time on making sense of the new information and little time on giving it relevance. By shifting the emphasis to relevance, students would more likely retain the learning at a higher rate.

Try the following tactics (Tileston, 2004c) to help students store and retrieve semantic information:

- Use nonlinguistic organizers, such as the mind map, to help students organize and remember the learning.

- Use peer teaching, in which students are paired with another student to review information. One of the ways to do this is to stop at intervals and ask students to tell each other what they remember from the information they have just been given.
- Put the information into manageable chunks by classifying or categorizing long lists.
- Use questioning strategies, such as Socratic questioning, to help students process the information.
- Make your room reflect the unit you are studying. Elementary teachers do a good job of this, but somewhere between middle school and high school this technique becomes lost. Just changing the room to reflect each unit helps the brain sort the information based on visuals present in the room when the information was learned.
- Wear hats or use symbols with the learning to help students remember. For example, I use picture frames when we are talking about frames of reference. Sometimes, when my students cannot remember, just saying, "Remember, it was on the blue picture frame" will help trigger the memory.
- Use mnemonics or stories to weave the information into memory. On a recent news show, students participating in the national memory contest were asked how they remember all the trivia and data they are given to memorize. One student said, "We weave a story around it to help us remember."
- Use music. Music leaves such a strong emotional impression on each of us. Bring in music to introduce and reinforce learning in the classroom.
- Use linguistic organizers to help your students with the learning. For example, to help students remember the various math concepts that you will study, you might provide an organizer, such as the one in Figure 4.2.

Figure 4.2 Matrix for Math Class

Math Unit	Formulas	Explanation	Example of Use

EPISODIC MEMORY

The second memory drawer in our file cabinet is *episodic*. Episodic memory is based on context and location. (Where were you when you learned the material, or in what context did you learn?) Sprenger (1999) uses the example of trying to remember where we were at the time of a traumatic event, such as the assassination of John F. Kennedy. According to her, students who learn information in one room and are tested in another tend to underperform. This has tremendous implications for giving standardized tests to students in the room in which they prepared for the test. Because episodic memory is attached to specific locations or contexts in which we first learned the material, students may look at a blank bulletin board when they are taking a test and in that way be able to remember the answer, since that is where the material was previously placed. As Sprenger (2002) tells us, "Although episodic details fade over time, they are excellent triggers for semantic memory information" (p. 81).

About 98 percent of all new information enters the brain through the five senses—taste, smell, hearing, sight, and touch. Most classrooms concentrate on hearing and sight (visuals), but we are finding that using the other senses helps to add extra "glue" to the learning. For example, while studying a time in history, try bringing in the sounds and smells associated with the time and place. Businesses already do this to increase sales. Try walking down the center of the mall—as you go by each store notice how they have used smells and sounds to get your attention. Once you are inside the store they use taste, smell, hearing, sight, and touch in many ways to hook you. Try placing one of those hanging scents made for cars in your classroom; studies are showing that students will associate the smell of your classroom with the learning. Try a scent such as chocolate—after class, even far removed from school, the smell of chocolate may very well reinforce the classroom work in the brain. This is a new area of science and learning but worth checking out.

Kay Toliver (1993), an outstanding teacher who has had so much success with teaching the at-risk children of Harlem, uses props to help students with learning. For a math lesson on multiplication, she comes to class with placards across the front and back of her torso that are replicas of a box of raisins. Her students worked with multiplication using raisins. What a great tool to help students when it comes time for recall on multiplication facts! Sprenger (1999) uses fact sheets printed on different colors of paper, depending on the subject of the fact sheets. When students are having trouble with recall, she mentions the color of the paper that contained the facts.

Try the following techniques (Tileston, 2004c) to help students make better use of the episodic memory system:

- Put information up so that it is visually accessible to the learners who need visuals to learn well. For English language learners, visuals are critical to their learning because they have limited semantic (language) acquisition strategies.

- Color code units or use symbols, especially if there is a great deal of vocabulary involved.
- Use graphic (nonlinguistic) organizers to help students "see" the learning and teach students to develop graphic organizers of their own for learning.
- Change the room arrangement prior to a new unit. This technique affects context ("Remember we talked about that information when you were all seated facing the windows").
- Use symbols and/or costumes to help students separate the learning. I use frames (frames of reference) when studying pollution. One group of students has a frame that says "politician," another group has a frame that says "new parent," another group has a frame that says "factory owner." Each group must talk about pollution according to the "frame of reference" they have been given. The frame serves as a *context* for the learning.

SENSORY MEMORY

Sensory memory is stored in the cerebellum, which is responsible for muscle coordination (Sousa, 2005). Processes such as driving a car are stored in this part of the brain. Rehearsal plays an important part in this memory. For example, I will not be able to remember how to drive a car unless I have practiced the process. If we want students to perform an operation easily, we must have them rehearse or perform the material often enough that it becomes procedural. One of Steven Covey's (1989) rules is called the *28-day rule.* Basically, the rule says that if you repeat a behavior for 28 days, it becomes internalized. Often used in changing behaviors, this rule draws on procedural memory to change negative thinking into positive by repetition. Jensen (1998) says that we enhance procedural memory through hands-on activities, manipulatives, role playing, and physical skills.

This system may be the strongest in terms of remembering. To make better use of this system, try adding movement to the learning in your classroom. This simple technique tends to give the content great strength in terms of storage and retrieval. Some teaching strategies (Tileston, 2004c) that seem to reinforce this system include the following:

- Role playing
- Drama
- Choral readings
- Projects
- Hands-on activities
- Manipulatives
- Debates
- Group activities

REFLECTIVE MEMORY

Reflective memory is triggered by stimuli. Any learning that has become automatic is stored in this pathway, for example, our conditioned responses such as how we react when we see a dog that we do not know. Whether we are fearful or happy to see the animal will depend on conditioned responses from past experiences. Emotions may be tied into this memory pathway, and indeed, how we respond to a song or a picture may very well come from this memory pathway based on reflective, unconscious learning or past experiences. Teachers from diverse classrooms who know their students are aware of the emotional responses that some stimulus may bring about in the classroom. For example, with Native American children, looking them in the eye may bring about the conditioned response of anger since within that culture it is offensive to make eye contact. The same is true for some Asian cultures. Knowing my students can help me as a teacher to avoid conflicts between my culture and the culture of my student.

MEASURING SUCCESS

Figure 4.3 shows the indicators that the strategies discussed in this chapter have been successfully implemented to help students store and access information in long-term memory.

Figure 4.3   Indicators of a Classroom in Which Teaching for Long-Term Memory Is a Primary Goal

Assessment Tool	Indicators of Success
Lesson plans	Include techniques to pique student interest in the learning: dynamic, of high interest, and presented in such a way that students are actively involved
Students' tasks and projects	Incorporate use of emotion, relevance, and high-interest materials
Student assessments	Include opportunities for reflection and self-assessment
Modifications for English language learners	Include graphics to help these students recall vocabulary and facts from the semantic memory system

CONCLUSION

The importance of memory is enormous; we use memory in every thought, every insight, and to make sense of our world. Mark Clayson puts it this way:

> The vast majority of us take memory for granted. We scarcely real-
> ize that memory is involved in nearly every single task we perform

each day in the world. The way memory works is related to such parts of the brain as the frontal lobe, the temporal lobe, the cortex, and the hippocampus. These disparate parts of the brain work together, thereby allowing us to formulate and store information in the form of memories. The memories connect us to the external world—the data stored might be about a specific environment, a person, or an object. (Clayson, 2007)

Understanding how we store and retrieve different types of information helps us as teachers to better understand why our students struggle with certain types of learning and how we can help them to make better use of the storage systems of the brain. We want to move students from simply memorizing information for the test on Friday and then promptly forgetting it to a system of learning that requires active participation by the brain, the use of visuals and processes, and meaningful rehearsal, with the goal of moving the learned content into long-term memory.

5

Constructing Knowledge Through Higher-Level Thinking Processes

Those who own the rights to inventions own the world.

—From the political platform of the
Japanese Democratic Party, as quoted by
Joseph Renzulli and Sally Reis (2008)

In a world that is changing exponentially, we cannot continue to try to pour facts into our students; there are just too many facts! Instead, we must begin to concentrate on ways to help students find information and then use it effectively. In his groundbreaking book, *A Whole New Mind*, Daniel Pink (2005) says that in the last century we modeled schools after factories in which people were experts on a small amount of facts learned linearly in order to do a specific job. We had facts that we believed were necessary to student success after they finished school, and we spent 12 years preparing them to know these facts in case they needed them.

Today, if students want to know a fact they "Google" it. What will be more important in this century (according to Pink) is to be able to be creative, be a problem-solver, and talk to anyone whether we agree with him or her or not. We live in an age of tremendous information that changes rapidly; if students are to be successful in life they must move beyond factual input to the processes involved in higher-level thinking such as problem solving, decision making, experimental inquiry, and investigation. We want to move students from the simple to the complex. I am not suggesting here that we give students more work or even that the work we give be more difficult; our aim is not to induce frustration or low motivation. But students today need complexity. These are students who can surf the Internet with ease and who can discuss a wide variety of universal topics. Simply giving them rote facts to memorize and give back on a test is boring. I don't need to know the names of state birds; I need to know how to find the names if I need them.

Sousa (2006) reminds us that there is a significant difference between complexity and difficulty. Complexity refers to the thought processes that the brain uses to deal with information. Difficulty, however, refers to the amount of effort expended within a level of complexity. A learner might expend a great deal of energy on difficulty while working at a low level of complexity. Sousa gives the example of requiring a student to name the states and their capitals in order of their admission to the Union. This example takes place on a low level of the hierarchy proposed by Marzano (2001a) but requires significant effort on the part of the student to memorize these facts. Factual knowledge is considered to be a low-level skill because the student does not even need to understand the information in order to prove she knows it; the student merely needs to be able to recite facts from a book.

While there is certainly nothing wrong with the just-mentioned assignment, students who are never allowed to go beyond this level or who expend so much effort at the low levels that they do not have time for the higher levels of thought are robbed of the opportunity to grow mentally. Teachers mistakenly think that slower students cannot work in the higher levels of the taxonomy, although studies show that the opposite is true. When these students are given only the critical attributes of the learning, without extraneous information to sort, they are able to perform at a more complex level. Sousa (2006) concludes that teachers can get slower students to be successful at the higher levels of learning if they review the curriculum, remove extraneous information and topics of least importance, and provide time for practice at the higher levels. We can move students to higher-level thinking by using scaffolding effectively. Scaffolding is structure that is added to the learning to help those students with learning gaps or understanding difficulties to be able to reach a level that they have not reached before. For example, suppose I want students to understand the differences in state and federal government. Here are the steps that I would take to get my students to the critical thinking necessary for a high-level skill.

1. First, we would learn the definitions of the federal and state governments, including their respective roles and scope of responsibilities.

2. Next, students would create attribute wheels, which show the attributes of each of the two levels of government (see Figure 5.1).

Figure 5.1 Levels of Government

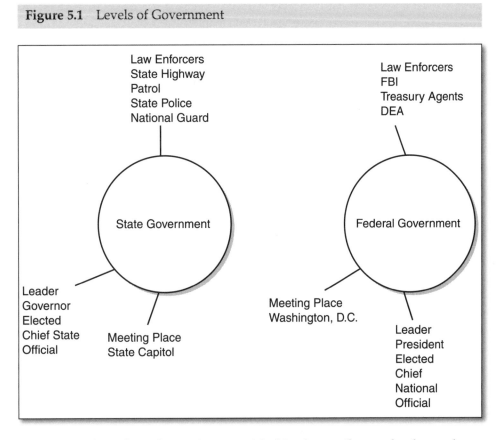

Law Enforcers
State Highway
Patrol
State Police
National Guard

Law Enforcers
FBI
Treasury Agents
DEA

State Government

Federal Government

Leader
Governor
Elected
Chief State
Official

Meeting Place
State Capitol

Meeting Place
Washington, D.C.

Leader
President
Elected
Chief
National
Official

3. Based on the information provided in the attribute wheels, students are ready to create a matrix like the one provided here.

State Government	Three ways they are alike: 1. Elected chief official 2. Meet in a designated capitol building 3. Have law enforcement agencies to carry out their work	**Federal Government**
Limited to state enforcement of laws passed by state legislature	Differences: level of power	Enforcement of federal laws that affect all states
State enforcement only by state highway patrol or emergency enforcement by the national guard	Differences: types of enforcement	Enforcement on a federal level by the FBI, U.S. Treasury, and DEA that includes all states
All laws enforced by highway patrol or state police. Only can use National Guard when a state of emergency has been declared.	Differences: level of enforcement	FBI regulates federal and constitutional law violations. Treasury agents enforce alcohol, tobacco, and firearms laws as well as fraud, forgery and counterfeiting. DEA enforces drug laws.

Once students have mastered attribute wheels and compare-and-contrast matrices, they can easily use the information to create Venn diagrams. They can also use this information to write a compare-and-contrast essay.

Using Marzano and Kendall's new taxonomy on educational objectives (2008), let's look at how we might move from very basic knowledge to more complex learning and process skills.

4. Retrieval objectives involve the recognition, recall, and execution of basic information and procedures.

5. Comprehension objectives involve identifying and symbolizing the critical features of knowledge.

6. Analysis objectives involve reasoned extensions of knowledge.

7. Knowledge utilization objectives are employed when knowledge is used to accomplish a specific task.

8. Metacognitive objectives address setting and monitoring goals.

9. Self-system objectives address attitudes, beliefs, and behaviors that control motivation. (p. 6)

Matching is the identification of similarities and differences between two or more things, people, components, facts, and so on. According to Marzano and Kendall (2008), the matching process contains these components:

- Specifying the attributes or characteristics on which items being matched are to be analyzed
- Determining how they are alike and different
- Stating similarities and differences as precisely as possible. (Figure 5.2 is an example of matching.)

Figure 5.2   Attribute Comparison Chart for Regular Nouns and Verbs

Noun	Attributes	Verb
Nouns may change spelling for plural form.	Spelling	Verbs change spelling for the third-person-singular form.
Proper nouns are capitalized no matter where they fall in the sentence.	Use of capitals	Verbs are only capitalized if they begin the sentence.
Nouns name a person, place, or thing.	What they name	Verbs name actions.
Nouns do not change tense.	Use of tense	Verbs change tense to show present, future, or past.

CLASSIFICATION

Students who can classify information understand how to use attributes to place things into categories. They also understand that things may go into more than one category. According to Marzano and Kendall (2008, p. 18), the components of the classifying process include the following:

- Indicating categories for the item and explaining how they are related
- Identifying the defining characteristics of the items to be classified
- Identifying a superordinate category to which the item belongs and explaining why it belongs in that category
- Identifying one or more categories
- Venn diagrams. These are often used when classifying items. Figure 5.3 utilizes a Venn diagram to compare and contrast two shapes—a square and a rectangle. Note that the left side of the diagram shows the attributes that are only true of rectangles; the right side identifies these attributes for squares. The center circle identifies common attributes. The figure shows the definitions, from Parks and Black (1992), of each of the shapes to help you as you examine the Venn diagram.

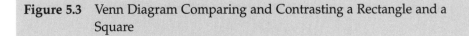

Figure 5.3   Venn Diagram Comparing and Contrasting a Rectangle and a Square

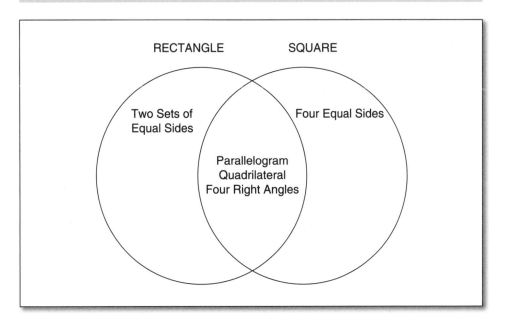

If your students have difficulty with Venn diagrams (which are showing up on state and national tests more frequently), begin with a comparison chart and then move them to Venn diagrams.

Marzano (1992) uses the following questions to assist students in using classification:

- Into what groups could you organize these things?
- What are the rules for membership in each group?
- What are the defining characteristics of each group?

INDUCTION

Induction is the ability to take what is known and predict what is not known. It is an important higher-level skill to assist students to make informed decisions about their world not only at this time but throughout life. We cannot teach students everything that they will have to know in life. What we can do is teach them these higher-order skills that can be applied to specific facts throughout life.

Consider this example. After studying the patterns of weather in Dallas, Texas, a student makes predictions about the weather in summer. In an inductive argument it is improvable that the conclusion will be false if the premises are true. Here's an example of an inductive argument:

- The average July temperature in Dallas is 98.
- I live in Dallas.
- I will experience very hot temperatures in July.

DEDUCTION

Deduction differs from induction in that induction is based on possible conclusions drawn by observation and facts; deduction is based on rules and principles that lead to absolutes. Induction deals with the unknown; deduction deals with what is known based on the principles involved. For example, in the Fibonacci sequence, the numbers 1, 2, 3, 5, 8 . . . are followed by 13. This is known because the rule is that the two numbers prior to the new number add up to the new number. Thus, we can deduce that the next number in the sequence is 13. Deduction only works if the premises are true. Here's an example of a deductive argument:

- All men are mortal.
- Abraham Lincoln was a man.
- Abraham Lincoln was mortal.

ERROR ANALYSIS

The ability to determine fallacy in thinking and to evaluate our own thinking and then the thinking of others is a skill worth developing. Because this involves personal evaluation, it is not necessarily a popular skill. Marzano (1992) recommends the following questions to aid with error analysis:

- What are the errors in reasoning in this information?
- How is this information misleading?
- How can it be corrected or improved?

CONSTRUCTING SUPPORT

Building support for ideas is a critical part of life. Students who learn the principles involved in skillfully being able to glean proof and support will have an important life skill as well as a tool that helps extend their knowledge. Persuasive writing is based on this ability. Marzano (1992) places constructing support into the following four categories, or "four appeals," developed by Kinneavy (1991):

1. *Appealing through personality.* Using this appeal, the speaker or writer has as his or her goal to be liked. This is usually done through personal information about the speaker or writer in the form of stories and anecdotes.

2. *Appealing through accepted beliefs and traditions.* The writer or speaker uses basic truths that are held by the audience to make a point. For example, "In Texas, this is the way we do things."

3. *Appealing through rhetoric.* By using language and gestures, the writer or speaker appeals to the audience.

4. *Appealing through logic.* The speaker or writer uses evidence, elaboration, and examples to win over the audience to his or her way of thinking. For example, "In this country, we produce enough food each year for every man, woman, and child in the world to have more than 2,500 calories per day. Why, then, do we have world hunger?"

ABSTRACTING OR PATTERN BUILDING

In Chapter 1, I discussed the fact that the brain likes and seeks patterns. The ability to create and understand patterns is an important skill in constructing meaning. Students who are adapt at this skill look for underlying causes and for ways that one phenomenon relates to another.

The second part to this type of thinking is the ability to see new patterns based on patterns that already exist. Linda Booth Sweeney's *When a Butterfly Sneezes* (2001) is built around patterns occurring in literature that can be applied to the real world. Ray Choiniere and David Keirsey, in *Presidential Temperament* (1992), ask the question, "If I know the mood of the country and the personality types of the presidential candidates, can I make an accurate prediction (based on past experiences) about who will win the election?"

ANALYZING PERSPECTIVES

Analyzing perspectives is the ability of the learner to view events and information from a perspective other than his or her own. Marzano (1992) suggests the following questions to analyze perspectives:

- Why would someone consider this to be good (or bad or neutral)?
- What is the reasoning behind their perspective?
- What is an alternative perspective, and what is the reasoning behind it?

The analysis level of the new taxonomy refers to higher-level thinking skills such as matching, classifying, analyzing, generating, and specifying that are important to student understanding and refinement of knowledge.

Matching. When students use matching they can use the process of compare and contrast from a simple example such as how a bicycle and a motorcycle are alike and different to more complex levels such as how fractions and decimals are alike and different. Knowing the key attributes that are important in determining how the items are different makes the task more complex. For example, in contrasting fractions and decimals, what is important? Converting the denominators? How they are represented?

Classifying. Students who can classify can put things into meaningful categories based on their attributes. To be able to do this effectively requires the ability to analyze why things go into certain categories. We can take this another level to forced categories that involve creativity. For example, things that are red might include a stop sign, lipstick, lips. We could then move into more creative categories like a newspaper or *The Red Badge of Courage.*

Analyzing. Students who can analyze errors can analyze the reasonableness or logic of a given statement and can find errors in thinking.

Generalizing. Students who can generalize effectively can find patterns or connections and can often explain those patterns when others have not made the connections. For example, a student studying *The Canterbury Tales* sees a pattern between the pilgrims who tell stories that in essence reflect very much about themselves and the characters he saw in an old rerun of a *Cheers* television show who meet after work and share stories.

Specifying. Students who can specify can find new applications to a given principle. In the last century we often said that the person who could invent a better mousetrap would be the one who was successful. In this century, according to Daniel Pink (2005), building a better mousetrap is not enough. It must be aesthetically pleasing and satisfy a problem that we have with the old version.

In the new taxonomy, knowledge utilization involves skills that allow us to accomplish tasks. To do this we must employ the high-level tasks of decision making, problem solving, experimenting, and investigating.

Students who can use decision-making tactics can determine the criteria on which the decision will be based, the alternatives, and the method for systematically making the decision.

Students who can problem solve can either overcome obstacles to a goal or can find alternatives to get around the obstacles. Marie Curie had difficulty as a female scientist because it was not appropriate for a woman to be a scientist at that time so she found an alternative way to get her findings out through her husband (for a time anyway).

Students who can use experimentation can create and successfully test a hypothesis. They can accurately evaluate the results as well.

Students who can investigate can test a hypothesis about past, present, or future events. For example, the pond in your neighborhood is suddenly polluted, and no other ponds in the area are, so students conduct an investigation to determine what has happened.

MEASURING SUCCESS

Figure 5.4 shows the indicators that will be present when higher-order thinking skills are a part of the learning.

Figure 5.4 Indicators of a Classroom in Which Higher-Level Thinking Skills Are Integrated Into the Lesson

Assessment Tool	Indicators of Success
Student products	Indicate that critical-thinking skills, creative-thinking skills, and problem-solving skills are encouraged and rewarded
Student products and assessments	Are at the analysis level of Bloom's taxonomy and above
Lesson plans	Indicate inductive thinking skills, such as cause and effect
Lesson plans	Indicate deductive thinking skills, such as logic and syllogisms
Student products	Indicate an understanding of the vocabulary of higher-order thinking skills
Student products	Indicate that students can perform the steps of complex problem solving

CONCLUSION

When higher-order thinking skills are a part of the learning, students use more complex thinking processes. Critical thinking, creative thinking, and problem solving should be encouraged and rewarded. As teachers, we should filter the material to be studied so that low-level and extraneous information are kept at a minimum to allow time for processing more complex skills. To the extent possible, student products and assessments should be at the analysis level or above. Inductive thinking skills, such as distinguishing cause and effect and making inferences, should be a part of the lesson plans, and students should be provided opportunities to use deductive thinking skills, such as logic and syllogistic thinking. All students should have the opportunity to work at higher levels, not just students identified as fast learners. When we do this, we raise the floor as well as the ceiling of achievement.

6

Fostering Collaborative Learning

In a world of ubiquitous information and advanced analytic tools, logic alone won't do it. We must be able to listen and to discern why people have come to the conclusions that they have, why they act as they do and why their thinking moves in a certain direction.

—Daniel Pink (2005, p. 66)

In his groundbreaking book, *A Whole New Mind*, Daniel Pink (2005) leads us into the twenty-first century with what he calls six senses that will help direct our minds to the demands of this century. Two of those new senses have to do with the ability to work with people, all people, whether we agree with them or not. In a world where we are competing globally this is essential. Pink says that we must learn to talk to people in the way that they understand best—by putting our thoughts and ideas into a story format. In this global world being able to argue a point is not enough because someone somewhere will be able to argue the point in another direction just as effectively. "The essence of persuasion, communication, and self-understanding has become the ability also to fashion a compelling narrative," Pink says (p.66).

The second sense that involves our ability to work with others, described in the quote just mentioned, is the ability to show genuine empathy and to understand others' thinking whether we agree with it or not. In the last century we put an emphasis on logic, but we no longer live in a world directed by logical thinking.

In my classrooms, even with my graduate students, I have always included collaborative learning. I tell my students up front that I want them to be the most marketable people in the workplace, and learning to work with other people is paramount to that. Collaboration is more than just working together in groups, however; it is the whole communication process in the classroom. How does the teacher communicate with students in regard to the information to be learned and how it is to be assessed? How do students communicate with the teacher and with each other? What is the role of the parent? Is the communication directed one way, two ways, or multiple ways? Is it in written, oral, tactile, or computer-generated form?

To be successful in the job market, students must be able to articulate what they know and to listen to the ideas and opinions of others. Students practice cooperative and collaborative learning strategies to help solidify what they have learned and to practice the learning so that when it is time for individual assessment, the learning is in long-term memory. Sizer (cited in O'Neil, 1995) says,

> The real world demands collaboration, the collective solving of problems . . . [and] learning to get along, to function effectively in a group is essential. Evidence and experience also strongly suggest that an individual's personal learning is enhanced by collaborative effort. The act of sharing ideas, of having to put one's own views clearly to others, of finding defensible compromises and conclusions, is in itself educative. (p. 12)

How can we ever expect students to learn the higher-level social task of criticizing ideas, not people, if they have not learned the basic task of collaborating effectively with others?

The Secretary's Commission on Achieving Necessary Skills (SCANS) report (U.S. Department of Labor, 1991) was an eye-opener at the time it was released because it said that while it is important for students to know reading, mathematics, and writing skills, one of the most important marketable skills that we can give students is the ability to work with other people. That information should have been no surprise since we have known for years that the primary reason why people lose jobs is not incompetence but the inability to get along with others. Students need classroom opportunities to work with everyone else in the classroom. Even very young children need social skills. It is one thing to know information; it is another dimension to be able to explain that information to someone else. Add to that the ability to do quality problem solving with small groups and you have a winning combination.

One of the most important marketable skills that we can give students is the ability to work with other people.

When we were working on research for our restructured school, one of our consultants visited with members of business and industry to ask first-hand what the important skills were that we should be teaching students. The overwhelming answer was that we should be teaching social and collaborative skills. One oil company executive said that, when prospective employees come in for an interview, the company brings them in small groups to the office. There, they are given a problem to solve. They are given a choice: they can work together on the solution, or they can work in cubicles to solve the problem alone. What the prospective employees do not know is if they choose to work alone, they will not be called back for a second interview. The Association of Supervision and Curriculum Development (ASCD) said in its 1999 yearbook, "The process of learning has passed from simple self-organization to collaborative, interpersonal, social problem-solving activity dependent on conversation, practical, meaningful involvement, and real world experience and application."

Cooperative learning has long been regarded as a "best practice" with today's students who have grown up with technology that allows them to be in touch with others 24/7. True cooperative learning is a process that involves specific actions such as homogenous groups and sitting eye to eye. When we look at data on effect sizes of cooperative learning it is important to recognize that in order to get those same effect sizes, we must use cooperative learning with all of the elements present. These elements include the following:

- *Reflection.* All students are provided the opportunity to reflect on their work in the cooperative groups.
- *Individual achievement.* Students discuss the learning together but are evaluated separately, not as a group.
- *Collaboration.* Thought has been put into the discussions and work of the cooperative groups. They have meaningful work that they share in the groups.
- *Higher-order thinking.* Cooperative learning is not busy work; it is high-level thinking and sharing.
- *Emotional realm.* Emotional bonds are encouraged.
- *Social skills.* Social skills are directly taught along with cognitive skills and are expected to be demonstrated within the groups.

Just putting people in groups is not enough. Marzano (2007) provides research results for using cooperative learning by several researchers. When looking at cooperative-learning studies of 122 effect sizes, they show that the average effect size of using this tool in the classroom is 0.73, or 27 percentile points. When students have an opportunity to discuss the learning with each other they not only are learning in a way that is brain-friendly to them, but they are advancing their own knowledge by hearing other opinions, watching body language and tone inflection, and developing a schema for remembering and making connections. It is also significant to add that these studies by Marzano show that the size of the groups is important as well. Groups of up to four show a percentile gain, but once the groups reach five and above, there is a negative gain.

Four primary communications are important to making collaborative learning significant in the classroom.

COMMUNICATION BETWEEN
THE TEACHER AND STUDENTS

In Chapter 1, the significance of the classroom environment and the power of a positive climate were presented. In the culturally responsive classroom, teachers are aware that for certain cultures it is important to create a relationship first. For Hispanic students not born in the United States and for African American students who were born and raised in the United States, it is essential to create a relationship first and then provide the substance of the lesson. Most teachers were taught in college to teach substance first and then create a relationship along the way. Thus many teachers have had negative experiences in diverse classrooms when they have not known or understood the importance of the relationship. Students from cultures that have had historically negative experiences with the descendants of Anglo-Saxon Northern Europeans (such as Native Americans and African Americans) may not trust the teacher who is of this heritage. We must take the time at the beginning of school to create a system of trust and mutual respect. Know the interests of your students and know their cultural backgrounds, including important customs and holidays.

The teacher sets the tone for the classroom through verbal and non-verbal communication. Not only is what is said to students important, but the tone and body movements are important as well. Jensen (2003) says that high stress and threat in the classroom impair brain cells. He goes on to say, "Threat also changes the body's chemistry and impacts learning." If students are made to believe that, no matter what they do, they cannot be successful in the classroom, threat exists. In Chapter 1, evidence was presented that the success of our students can be dramatically raised just by saying to them that we will not let them fail and then backing that up with actions. Jensen (2003) provides these additional examples of threat in the classroom:

- Anything that embarrasses students in front of their peers
- Unrealistic deadlines or demands such as giving assignments without the necessary resources, support, or information
- A student's inability to speak a language. Remember that English language learners usually understand what is being said sooner than they are willing to speak out loud for fear of being laughed at for their pronunciations.
- Uncomfortable classroom cultures such as a room that only reflects the dominant culture
- A bully in the hallway, the playground, or on the computer
- Inappropriate learning styles, especially for students who struggle with the learning. For these students we must reteach in the modality most comfortable to the brain.
- Speaking in a threatening tone
- Out-of-class factors, such as a fight with family members

When threat exists, the brain operates in survival mode, and while we can learn in that mode, we do so at the expense of higher-order thinking. In addition, threat keeps us from being in a state of well-being. In his book on the states of the brain, Jensen (2003) says that humans are capable of being in the state of well-being longer than any other state. Why, then, are some people often out of that state? The reason is that threats, emergencies, distress, and other distractions keep them from the more desirable state of mind. He goes on to say that this state of well-being is important because "when our serotonin levels are just right we feel neither dominant nor subordinate. When our energy levels are just right, we are neither bounding off the walls nor drowsy" (p. 101).

Once a positive climate has been established, the teacher must *communicate expectations verbally and in writing.* Why both? In a diverse classroom, some students will need the information in writing while others will prefer to hear the information. Expectations include classroom rules as well as learning expectations. Prior to any assignment in which students will be assessed, they should be told verbally and in writing what they have to do to be successful—and that should be followed to the letter. When we tell students in advance what it takes to be successful, we take away the "gotchas." There are no surprises: students know in advance how they will be assessed, whether through a rubric or through some other written communication. These rubrics should be specific. When we make them specific, we help level the playing field so that everyone starts with the same opportunity for success. In the diverse classroom this is critical since students may not understand what you mean by a "quality product" or "personal best" unless you specifically tell them what that looks like.

Teachers must also *set realistic benchmarks,* which includes frequent intervals to check for student understanding. These should be interspersed within the class day or period. Sousa (2006) says that assessment for a grade should not come until 24 hours after learning, because we cannot be sure that the information is in long-term memory until at least that amount of time has passed. Benchmarks, however, refer to making sure the students understand—not to assessment for grades.

Effective communication between students and teacher also requires what I call *cruise control.* As a teacher, I cruise the room while my students are working so that I know on an ongoing basis who is off task, who doesn't understand, and who is in danger of failing. When one of these factors is present, I can intervene immediately.

Last, the teacher must begin to take on the role of coach, leader, or guide in the classroom to stir the students by dynamic, interesting presentations of the learning that allow them to participate actively. The teacher cannot continue to be the lecturer with the students as passive listeners. Students today come from a sound-bite world that constantly bombards the senses. They will not—they cannot—sit all day as passive listeners. Jensen (1998) says, "Today's teachers must think of themselves as a catalyst for learning, not a live, breathing textbook. Schools simply must have greater roles, like creating motivated, thinking, responsible, and productive citizens for the next century."

STUDENT-TO-STUDENT COMMUNICATION

Jensen (1998) says,

> Our brain cannot be good at everything, therefore, it selects over time that which will ensure its survival. As a species, the human brain has evolved to use language as our primary means for communication. This may partly explain why groups, teams and cooperative learning benefit our understanding and application of new concepts; group work requires us to communicate with each other. Through this process, learning seems to be enhanced. (p. 82)

We learn best when we teach something to someone else. As a teacher, when did you know your subject best? Probably when you taught it to someone else. We need to make use of this powerful teaching technique by giving students opportunities to tell about the learning.

Students also need the opportunity to work with other people—not just their best friends. Social skills, group interaction skills, conversation skills, and group problem-solving skills are some of the highest-level skills we can give to our students. These abilities may have more to do with their success in life than the academic skills we give them. They certainly have a great deal to do with their finding satisfying and rewarding relationships—both personal and collegial. For teachers who have not attempted group activities in the past but are convinced it is worth trying, I offer the following guidelines:

- Start small—begin by letting students work in pairs for a short amount of time. The ideal time to use this would be after presenting information for 15 to 20 minutes, during the 10 minutes of downtime. Have students discuss what has been said, formulate questions about the new material, or use the information in some way. Not only does this produce social skills, but it also helps solidify the new learning.
- The first few times that students are put into small groups, use familiar material. A unit you have never taught before is not a good time to try group work for the first time.
- Make sure that any assigned group work is meaningful. Students know when it is busy work and will react accordingly.
- Time all activities and stick to the time schedule. Allow only enough time for the groups to do the work effectively—push the envelope a little. If you tell students they have eight minutes to complete an activity and you give them 15, they will not take the time limit seriously the next time.
- Tell students up front why they are working in small groups. Tell them it is an important real-world skill and you want them to be highly successful in whatever they do. Tell them it is a privilege

to get to work with other people instead of doing all the work alone. Tell them about synergy.

- Sign up for instruction in cooperative-learning techniques. You will learn a great deal about how to set up groups and manage them.

Cooperative learning, when used correctly, has an effect size equal to 27 percentile points. Here is an example of inquiry or group investigation, a cooperative-learning strategy that incorporates group sharing:

> *Students study together a problem or phenomena provided by the teacher. For example, a science teacher might say that the neighborhood pond is suddenly polluted and that the students will be investigating to determine the cause. Next, students explore the reactions to the problem. Are people in the neighborhood surprised? Has this ever happened before? Students then put together a plan for determining the cause of the pollution. Students will have roles that they will play as a group and individually. For example, the group may want to visit the pond or send out one or two members to gather information. Someone may want to interview people in the neighborhood. The teacher and the students will review the data and the evidence so far and will adjust their plan accordingly.*

Students who participate in this manner are learning important high-level skills such as investigation, data collection and analyzation, and how to test a hypothesis. Because they are communicating with one another they are learning how others think and draw conclusions, and they are learning to share information. In most cultures of the world this is a highly prized ability. When inquiry is implemented effectively it can have a 37 percentile effect on student learning (Tileston & Darling, 2008b).

COMMUNICATION WITH PARENTS

Letters, notes, e-mail, phone calls, parent conferences, and group meetings are essential to maintaining a positive climate. In our restructured school, we had a VIP (Very Important Parents) Committee. This committee helped create an open-door policy for parents and was the catalyst for setting up parent meetings—both individual and group. Parents were welcome in the school and encouraged to sit in on classroom lessons at any time. Our only requirement was that the parents sign up in advance with our VIP chairperson. This last requirement was for safety, so that we always knew who was in our building. An interesting thing happens when parents are in classrooms and hallways: Discipline problems are diminished. An added benefit is that those parents become advocates in the community. We never held staff development sessions that parents were not invited to attend. I believe that is why we were able to make such radical changes in such a short amount of time. Anytime someone in the community said, "I don't know what they are doing at that school," there was someone who had been to the meetings, to the school, or in the training who could speak for us. In tough economic times, it is essential that we find ways to communicate with parents outside of regular class time. Most parents are working today, and some are working more than one job just to make ends meet. Because they do not come to school we should not assume that they do not care about their child's education. Most parents care a great deal but may be either at work or simply not able to come to the school at the hour that we set meetings or open house. As I work in inner-city schools, I have found that even in high-poverty areas parents often tell us to send information electronically since most workplaces today have access to computers.

COMMUNICATION BETWEEN THE TEACHER AND OTHER STAFF MEMBERS

Teachers need the opportunity to work with each other just as students do. It is difficult to set a positive classroom climate if the climate outside the classroom is negative. Unless the administration is supportive, teachers will have a difficult time creating a collaborative environment. I have known situations where teachers created a collaborative environment with an unsupportive administration, but the individual teachers spent many exhausting and frustrating days and nights to make it happen.

In our restructured school, teachers met daily in small teams to discuss a variety of topics. This time was built into the school day. Each team of teachers was responsible for 100 students. They were responsible for seeing whether any of them were absent too often, having discipline problems, or in danger of failure. Students with problems were called in to meet with the whole team. Teachers also discussed assignments for the week.

It is difficult to understand why some nights kids have no homework, and other nights they are stressed over an unrealistic amount of work. Communication can help solve that problem. Teachers who meet daily can discuss upcoming assignments and work together on making them more evenly spaced. This is also the way to integrate learning. There are so many natural ways to connect one subject to another—*natural* meaning that the connection is already there, that it does not have to be forced. In our restructured school, the more integrations we made, the more we found. As a result, math, science, English, and social studies became naturally aligned.

With the importance of response to intervention and the mandates of federal laws, it is imperative that teachers communicate as never before to create workable plans to prevent failure early so that we do not have students who are incorrectly placed into special education or who are allowed to fail before we intervene. Only through good communication can we make RTI work.

MEASURING SUCCESS

Figure 6.1 shows the indicators that will be present when multiple communication channels are present in the classroom.

Figure 6.1 Indicators of a Classroom in Which Collaboration Is an Integral Part of the Learning

Assessment Tool	Indicators of Success
Observations	Indicate that interaction is a part of the classroom and include higher-order thinking skills, such as making distinctions, applying ideas, forming generalizations, raising questions, and not just reporting experiences, facts, definitions, or procedures
Observations	Indicate that the teacher acts as a catalyst to the learning, not as a living textbook
Lesson plans and observations	Indicate that students are provided numerous opportunities to work together to practice the learning, develop concepts, discuss ideas, and produce quality products
Observations	Mutual respect will be evident in the verbal and nonverbal communication of the teacher and the students.
Observations, student products	Students will be actively engaged, not passive receivers of the information.
Observations, student assessment	There is an expectation that students will master social skills.
Projects and assignments	Clearly indicate that effective collaboration has taken place
Climate surveys	Indicate that teachers and administration have active, ongoing communication
Parent surveys	Indicate that parents feel they are a part of the process; an open-door policy exists to allow parents to visit the classroom and communicate with teachers and staff

CONCLUSION

Where multiple channels of communication are present in the classroom, interaction will be evident. Students will be actively discussing tasks with the teacher and with each other. In addition, in a classroom where communication is multidirectional, the teacher will act as a catalyst to the learning, not as the living textbook. Newmann and Wehlage (1993) add, "Sharing of ideas is evident in exchanges that are not completely scripted or controlled (as in a teacher-led recitation). Questions are asked in complete sentences and responses are made to the comments of other speakers." Students will be provided numerous opportunities to work together to practice the learning, develop concepts, discuss ideas, and produce quality products. Mutual respect will be evident in the verbal and nonverbal communication of the teacher and the students. Students will be actively engaged, not passive receivers of the information. Moreover, risk taking will be encouraged and supported. Teachers as well as students will be risk takers with the learning. Social skills will be a part of the learning and the assessment process. SCANS (U.S. Department of Labor, 1991) puts collaborative skills right up there with math and reading, so they should be given importance in the classroom, not just because they are a skill for the marketplace but also because they are a skill for life. Projects and assignments should clearly indicate that effective collaboration has taken place.

Teachers and the administration should have active, ongoing communication with parents as an integral part of the process. In this multiply communicative school, every day is open house, for an open-door policy will exist that allows parents to visit the classroom and to communicate with teachers and staff whenever needed.

7

Bridging the Gap Between All Learners

Culture is broadly defined as a common heritage or set of beliefs, norms, and values. It refers to the shared and largely learned attributes of a group of people.

—U.S. Department of Health and
Human Services (2001)

The time has come to stop assuming that all students come to us with the scaffolding in place to be successful in school. They do not. One has only to look at the data on student success to know that we are not making much progress with reaching poor children. Figure 7.1, for example, shows the growth of the number of students from poverty and minority races placed into special education each year. Notice that while the overall enrollment in schools is declining in this country, the enrollment of special education is increasing. Could it be that schools today are still teaching to the dominant culture of the past rather than to the students today? There are many articles and books in the field that discuss the reasons why this is true, so I will not spend time here rehashing what we already know. Instead, I want to offer the following solutions based on the research and data available.

Figure 7.1 Changes in the Number of Children From Poverty and Minorities in Special Education

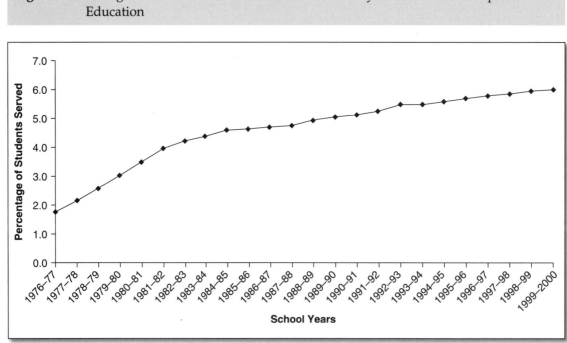

WE MUST PROVIDE POOR CHILDREN WITH THE VERY BEST TEACHERS AVAILABLE

For as long as I can remember we have told children to get a good education—that it is their key to success in life. But as Carmen Arroyo put it in her article on funding gaps in schools for the poor, many states do not provide the opportunity for poor students to get a quality education. "Despite national imagery full of high-flying concepts like 'equal opportunity' and 'level playing field,' English learner, low-income and minority students do not get the extra school supports they need to catch up to their more advantaged peers; they all too frequently receive less than do other students" (Arroyo, 2008, p. 1).

Education Trust (Arroyo, 2008) examined the spending patterns of each state from 1999 to 2005 to determine if there were spending gaps between the schools serving the largest number of students from poverty and the schools serving the lowest number of these students. The report also looked at the spending patterns between schools with high concentrations of students who were English language learners and those that were not. The results showed that, for the most part, we tend to spend more on students who do not live in poverty and on students who speak English as their first language. It means that we may be spending less on the students who actually need the most help—the most vulnerable. The chart that follows shows the accumulation of data for 2004–2005 between state and local funding in high- versus low-poverty districts.

Criteria	Number of States
Spent more dollars per student in high-poverty districts	18
Spent about the same per student	15
Spent less per student in high-poverty districts	16

Based on this data, only 18 of the 49 states studied provide additional funding for these students with the greatest needs. Thirty-one of the states do not. Hawaii was not a part of the study because it operates as a single statewide district.

This same report showed that only 14 of 49 states spend more per student in high-minority districts where poverty, inferior preschool programs, and greater health risks are usually factors. Last, of the eight states with the highest concentration of English language learners, only one state spent more per student to educate these students.

The report released by Education Trust (Arroyo, 2008) took a hard look at the state of Texas for patterns of inequity in teacher quality. I want to point out that while Texas was the state used in the study, the same data is true of other states as well. The report examined the 50 largest school districts in Texas and found that students in Texas who were Hispanic, African American, and of low income did not get their fair share in education. The report showed the following:

- These students are less likely to be assigned to teachers who are fully credentialed.
- These students are less likely to be in classrooms with experienced teachers.
- These students are less likely to attend schools with a stable teaching force.
- The average teacher salary in low-income schools was less.

I worked in a large-city school district that had an unwritten rule: "If you mess up, your punishment will be that you will be transferred to a poor school." I wonder how many schools across the country adhere to that same rule. We need to reverse that thinking. Make it a reward to work with children from diverse backgrounds by providing teachers with the structures they need to be successful. Namely, give teachers outstanding training on working with diverse learners; provide them with facilities, technology, and materials that rival the best schools; and provide a support system for those days when things do not go well. Think of a building with scaffolding adequate to withstand anything—even strong winds. We must give these teachers the scaffolding to be successful.

We must enable teachers so that failure is not an option for them either. The passage of mandates without sufficient funding or teacher training to carry them out has been counterproductive. It is interesting that both IDEA

(Individuals with Disabilities Education Act) 2004 and No Child Left Behind require teachers to use research-based best practices but do not say what those practices are, nor do they provide for the professional development that would help schools put them into place. The No Child Left Behind legislation (2002) offers as goals "holding schools, local education agencies, and States accountable for improving the academic achievement of all students" and "promoting schoolwide reform and ensuring the access of all children to effective, scientifically-based instructional strategies" (PL 107–110 & 1001(4) and (9)). The goal of IDEA (2005) is "to improve the academic achievement and functional performance of children with disabilities including the use of scientifically based instructional practices, to the maximum extent possible" (20U.S.C. 1400©(5)(E)). Never before has so much emphasis been placed on the use of practices proved to be effective. There are consequences for poor achievement but little guidance on how teachers can put their knowledge and experience to work in the classroom more effectively. It is no wonder that so many teachers are frustrated with the lack of self-efficacy associated with these laws and regulations.

WE MUST PROVIDE A HIGH-QUALITY AND CHALLENGING CURRICULUM FOR EVERY STUDENT

Every student deserves a quality education; in a century in which students will be competing in a global marketplace anything less is malpractice. You may be saying, "But so many children from poverty come without the skills necessary to be successful in the classroom." It's true that children from poverty usually have access to lower-quality preschool programs than do those from higher incomes and thus do not come with the same level of enriched experiences. They usually don't have the vocabulary skills of their counterparts and may be placed into special programs by educators who mistakenly think the lack of vocabulary (and thus reading readiness skills) is neurological rather than due to lack of exposure. Response to Intervention is an attempt to change that process, but it has a long way to go before it will close the floodgates for students being incorrectly placed in programs in which they do not belong.

Educators made an assumption in the last decade that if they just made kids feel good about themselves and the teacher, all would be well. They would achieve at a high level regardless of race, creed, ethnicity, and poverty level. The way to get to that point, many educators believed, was to "water down" the curriculum in order to provide more opportunities for success. While it is important that students feel good about the classroom, subject, and teacher, there is nothing about watering down the material that makes students feel better about themselves: just the opposite.

There is nothing about watering down the material that makes students feel better about themselves.

We must make quality learning equitable, and one of the fundamental ways to accomplish this goal is to foster the literacy skills, broadly defined, of all our students. In our book *Closing the Poverty and Culture Gap*, my colleague Sandra Darling and I share four key ways that we must promote literacy in this decade:

1. *Academic literacy.* Many times teachers will say that they cannot provide academic literacy when the students are so far behind. We can provide this type of literacy to all students regardless of the academic gaps if we provide structures or scaffolding to assist them in creating mental models and in making sense of the learning. Teachers must be trained in a minimum of the following: (1) employing brain-compatible instructional strategies, (2) embedding culture into curriculum and instructional practices, (3) knowing and using effective, research-based instruction, (4) making technology an integral part of the teaching/learning experience, (5) rethinking assessment, (6) fostering high-level thinking and creativity, (7) using collaboration effectively, (8) bringing real-world applications to the learning, (9) developing twenty-first-century literacy skills, and (10) making resiliency an everyday goal (Tileston & Darling, 2009, p. 77).

2. *Cultural literacy.* In a culturally responsive classroom both the dominant culture and the cultures of the students are reflected in the work, materials, curriculum, and celebrations of the learning. Teachers know their students and seek to know the background knowledge prior to introducing new information or skills. Teachers expect that there will be respect for all cultures in the classroom, and they lead the way by examining their own biases and values and then by treating all children equitably.

3. *Social literacy.* In a classroom where social literacy is valued the teacher is aware of the value systems of the various cultures in the classroom and takes these into account in the instructional strategies that are used daily.

4. *Emotional literacy.* Being emotionally literate means that we can control our emotions, actions, and reactions to others. It also means that we are resilient. When we build resiliency in our students from poverty, we provide them with a caring and supportive relationship, high expectations with no excuses, and opportunities to actively participate in learning to overcome adverse conditions and be successful (Tileston & Darling, 2009, p. 78).

WE MUST UNDERSTAND THE CULTURE OF OUR STUDENTS

Bonnie Benard (2003) defines the social competence of students in a diverse classroom this way: "Social competence consists of relationship skills. It involves responsiveness, especially the ability to elicit positive responses from others; flexibility, including the ability to move back and forth between primary culture and dominant culture (cross-cultural competence); and empathy, caring, communication skills, and a sense of humor" (p. 99).

Children from poverty often enter public schools alongside children from middle-class and affluent backgrounds who have had enriched experiences to prepare them for the classroom and learning. In other words, for many students the entrance to public schools is not a door but already a sorting device that determines the future of their schooling. It is not that these students can't learn or won't learn; they often have not had the opportunities to learn. I am not just talking about learning the names of colors, ABCs, and how to count. I am talking also about setting goals, knowing what to do when things are not working, and understanding how to get along in a middle-class atmosphere. Public education is built around middle-class values, attitudes, and rules. Until this country begins to examine and structure early childhood programs so that every child in America has the opportunity to have rich experiences in day care, the gap will always begin at this early stage.

To provide a bridge for students, there are some factors that must be present; first we must get away from isolation practices. I have been in more than a few classrooms where minority students or students whose primary language is different are seated at the back of the room, isolated from the rest of the classroom. Move their desks to the front of the room and in proximity to the other students. They need the interaction and the attention.

We tend to classify people into social groups based on characteristics such as race and ethnicity (LAB at Brown University, 2001). When we do this, we often make an assumption that one race is superior to others. We call this racism; assumptions are often made about children from other races who come to the classroom with instructional gaps due to educational experiences that do not match our expectations. Schools sometimes treat these children as though they need to be "fixed" or made to conform to the dominant culture. According to Clauss-Ehlers, "Ethnicity is a cultural heritage that encompasses language, history, and rituals that are passed from one generation to the next. Ethnicity refers to a shared national or religious identity" (Clauss-Ehlers, 2006, p. 50). These heritages that our students bring with them need to be embraced in our classrooms.

As educators we need to first examine our own belief systems about students. Do we judge students based on appearance? And we must make sure that the curriculum reflects diverse racial and ethnic backgrounds. I often provide a test for my students based on Gardner's multiple intelligences (1993). We all have strengths and weaknesses; help students to see their areas of giftedness—we all tend to have two or three areas that are strong. By doing this we are moving away from a deficit model that looks only at gaps to an abundance model that asks first, "What are the gifts that you bring?"

Second, we must build relationships. For students from most cultures outside the Northern European model, it is important to build relationships first and then provide the substance of the learning. This can be accomplished by creating a community of learners who are treated consistently and fairly and who are given the tools needed to be successful. Teachers who have high expectations, and believe all kids can and must learn, will be more able to build these relationships.

Third, we must teach students the social skills they will need to be successful in the world they will enter. Part of the reality is that different cultures are taught to react differently in stressful situations. Children from generational poverty are taught to laugh in the face of adversity so that they do not show fear. A student who laughs when disciplined, however, will face further discipline. Schools tend to be built around middle-class standards that require a change in behavior and contriteness after discipline. I do not advocate that we accept middle-class standards unthinkingly, but I do believe that we need to educate students about expected behavior. Sometimes we must teach a dual cultural survival—one for out of school and one at school. For example, children raised on the land of Native Americans with strong ties to the tribe often believe that when they are looked in the eye it is an insult. A teacher from a Native American school told me that some of his students who went to college were in trouble the first week for confronting other students who looked them in the eye. Helping students to know the mores of the dominant culture is sometimes a way to prevent them from failure. At the same time we want them to honor their culture and to be the person they are.

Fourth, we must take a hard look at assessments to identify students who are at risk of academic underachievement due to skill gaps in the learning; and we must intervene early to close those gaps. Often, when scores are high for a group, the low scores of a single, small group can be masked. Programs like Response to Intervention are making progress in identifying struggling students. But as teachers we can make sure that the students in our classrooms don't have to wait to fail to get the interventions that they need. Put students with the same kinds of skill gaps in small groups so that they can receive additional tutoring to close gaps in the learning.

Fifth, where the cognitive structures are not in place, we must take the time to provide them. I have already discussed the importance of building brain connections (see Chapter 3). We cannot assume that any student already has the cognitive structure in place to connect to new learning. We can help by providing scaffolding for the learning while the gaps are being filled. Using visual models is one important way to do this; for example, don't just teach the principles of mathematics; show students visually how the math works. Many students, including those from poverty and English learners, learn better by seeing and doing than by sitting and listening. For example, in her wonderful book, *Painless Algebra,* Lynette Long (2006) puts math into the English language. Think about it. Mathematics has its own language, and many students struggle because they do not know or understand the language. A typical question on a high-stakes test asks students to look at the examples provided and choose the number that is a prime number. In order to correctly answer the question, I must know what is meant by the term "prime number." One of the things that I love about Long's book is that she not only helps students to understand the language of math, but she shares mistakes that are often made so that students know what to do and what not to do. For example, after teaching about addition and the fact that it does not matter what order the numbers are in to arrive at the sum, she warns about applying the same rule to subtraction. She first notes that "if I add 3 + 5, I will get the same answer that I would get if I added 5 + 3." Then she adds, "Caution—Major Mistake Territory! Subtraction is not commutative. The order of the numbers in a subtraction problem does make a difference. 6 − 3 is not the same as 3 − 6. 5 − 0 is not the same as 0 − 5" (p. 24).

WE MUST FIND WAYS TO BUILD SELF-EFFICACY

Not all students come to us with the scaffolding in place to be successful. They may not have the language acquisition skills to be able to put factual information into long-term memory. (The semantic memory system relies on words—if I do not know and understand the words, I will either not store the information or will store it in such a way that I cannot retrieve it.) They may not know the hidden rules of the middle class upon which public schools operate. They may not know how to set goals or what to do when a goal is not working out. Students who do not know how to plan and adjust will acquiesce at the first sign of trouble. That is why we get students who begin a project or work assignment but do not finish.

We must directly teach students the skills necessary to be successful. Self-efficacy is the belief that I can do something because I have encountered success in the past—that I have the necessary information, resources, and support to be successful. When we do not give students our instructional expectations up front, when we test on items that were not taught or that were not taught well, or when we do not directly teach the skills necessary to carry out the assignment, we limit self-efficacy in our classrooms. Provide students with the goals for the learning, lead them to set personal goals for their own learning, give them a matrix that shows them what they have to do to be successful, and test what you teach. It is a simple formula for success that is proven. Students from poverty often believe that they have a low locus of control, that bad things happen to them due to luck or some force that they cannot control. As a child of poverty myself, I often hear my father say, when something goes wrong, "It's just the Walker luck!" We have to directly teach students that most of the things that happen to us are based on cause and effect, not blind luck.

WE MUST BE RABID ABOUT ELIMINATING BIAS

In my book *What Every Teacher Should Know About Diverse Learners* (Tileston, 2010), I talk about the types of bias outlined by Gibbs (1994). For the purposes of this book, I will provide the list of categories as I've defined them and a brief explanation of each.

- *Linguistic bias.* Linguistic bias includes any behavior that is dehumanizing or denies the existence of a certain group. This includes laughing at students' names or teaching history without acknowledging the contributions of minorities. Teachers of English language learners tell me that their students can usually speak more English words than they may be willing for us to know about. They may not speak or read aloud in the classroom for fear of laughter due to their accents.

- *Stereotyping.* Stereotyping is a form of bias that occurs when we assume that a given set of criteria apply to all members of a group. This includes representations of minorities in supporting roles rather than leadership roles, of females with limits on what professions they can enter, and of disabled students as helpless. Look at books, materials, and visuals used in the classroom and remove those that reinforce such biases. Beware also of representations that lump together different groups. There are many cultures within any given race, and there are cultures that go across racial boundaries. A Hispanic or Latino student who was born in Mexico may not have the same cultural values and beliefs as a Hispanic student born in Cuba or South America. For that matter, a Hispanic student who lives on the border of Texas will probably be very different culturally from a Hispanic student who lives in Iowa and only travels back to Mexico once a year.

- *Exclusion.* Exclusion is the lack of representation from a group. It can also be the removal of a group from the larger group based on race, ethnicity, religion, or gender. At one time in this country, students who learned in a different modality from the teaching or who came to school without the prerequisite skills were placed in Title I or special education programs incorrectly. Data from the federal government in regard to Response to Intervention shows that we are still doing this for students who are different from the dominant group in the classroom. We have terribly skewed numbers of students from poverty and from minority groups in special education—far beyond the normal percentages we would expect. We call these students instructional casualties because the problem is not with them; it is with the system that does not know how to assess and teach them appropriately.

- *Unreality.* Unreality is the misinformation about a group, event, or contribution. We do this when we lower our expectations for students based on preconceived ideas, such as how their siblings did in our classrooms.

- *Selectivity.* Selectivity is the single interpretation of an issue, situation, or condition. We do this when we fail to understand the cultural backgrounds of our students and assume that all students will come to us with middle-class values and understandings.

- *Isolation.* Isolation is the separating of groups. It takes place when grouping centers around all-male or all-female groups or groups based on factors such as ethnicity or race.

WE MUST WORK WITH PARENTS AND COMMUNITY LEADERS

Poverty is not just lack of wealth; it is lack of services as well. Tileston (2004a) says,

> The solutions are not confined to the schools, but must be a part of a unified effort on the part of national, state, and local entities that work hand in hand with parents and the school. In order for poor students to be able to compete on a level playing field, they must have the quality health, nutrition, and other resources that are a part of the package of essentials provided to children who do not come from poverty. (p. 62)

Wang and Kovach (1996) agree: "Narrowly conceived plans and commitment that focus only on schools will not solve the growing problems that must be addressed to ensure success of the many children and youth who have not fared well under the current system of service delivery."

For so long, educators have often made the mistake of thinking that parents who do not come to school for meetings or to attend functions do not care about their kids. Most parents care very much about the education of their children. Most parents of poor children work long and often inconsistent hours (such as shift work) that does not allow for them to attend meetings or functions. More and more, in a down economy, parents are taking on more work or second jobs in order to meet their financial obligations. Parents who are in this country on temporary status or who have come from countries where authority is feared may be afraid to come to school for fear that they will be deported or that something will happen to them or their child. Look for alternatives to communicating with parents such as websites, letters, and to the extent possible put information in their first language. Before a new unit tell parents how they can reinforce the learning at home. Start a "Parent Ideas" newsletter to help parents reinforce the learning with their children at home.

We need to be strong advocates for parental support in the communities in which we teach. Begin with the leaders of the community. Set up parent groups to help you achieve the goals of your classroom and school. One of my schools has a committee called the VIP (Very Important Parents) Committee, which heads up school open houses, parent committees, school functions, and so forth. They have taken some of the work off of teachers and have been able to get parents to school when the best efforts of the school personnel have failed.

Help students find and use needed medical and social services. Be an advocate for helping organizations join hands to provide much-needed services for these students.

WE MUST CHANGE OUR WAY OF THINKING

There was a time in this country when educators assumed that only a few students would be successful. This type of thinking was based on the bell curve model. Some would be successful, some would fail, and the majority would fall somewhere in the middle. Later, through the work of psychologists such as Benjamin Bloom, we came to understand that more children would be successful if given more time, resources, and so forth. The saying of the time was, "All kids can learn." Today, we know not only that all kids can learn but also that they *must* learn. We cannot afford a generation that does not read, cannot do basic math, and cannot articulate their ideas to others.

We will not change the dynamics of poverty until we do something about education. This means that we must begin now to provide a quality preschool program for the poor and must utilize that time to help provide the scaffolding needed to be successful in school from the beginning. While that scaffolding includes a knowledge of letter sounds, a familiarity with numbers, and a love for books, that is only part of the underpinning. We must teach children how to plan, how to use self-talk, and what to do when plans are not going well. We must instruct them in the hidden rules upon which school and work depend. We must directly teach them the vocabulary of the classroom and find accurate ways to assess both their weaknesses and strengths. It is time to stop looking at children from poverty as kids who need to be "fixed." Let's fix the system instead. We begin by helping them to see their strengths rather than their weaknesses, and we must directly teach them cause and effect. So many children from poverty believe that they have no locus of control; that bad things always happen to them and to their family. We have to reverse that thinking and help them to understand that most things happen because of our own actions and choices.

MEASURING SUCCESS

Figure 7.2 shows the indicators that will be present when all students are successful.

Figure 7.2   Indicators That the Gap Between All Learners Has Been Bridged

Assessment Tool	Indicators of Success
Test Data	Data will be analyzed for trends, highs, lows, and each represented group. The tests will be appropriate for the students being tested—and be bias free.
Observations	Relationships will be a priority in the classroom. Most teachers from a Northern European background have emphasized substance first, relationships second. We must reverse the trend.
Student Products	Student products indicate that instruction has been designed to solicit, incorporate, and build upon the knowledge, experiences, and perspectives of all students.
Staff Training	Staff training indicates that teachers stay abreast of latest trends and methodologies for all student groups. Teachers have cultural literacy skills.

CONCLUSION

We have more than 3 million children who live in poverty in the wealthiest and most advanced country in the world. We know from the research that students of color and from poverty are being placed into special education programs at unprecedented numbers. We know that African American males have a 59 percent chance of dropping out of school and that one out of four will have spent time in prison or on a suspended sentence before the age of 25. In the meantime, three out of four white males will have gone to college (Rank, 2005, p. 159). Children from poverty come to school with half the vocabulary of the other students—and without interventions, they will have only one-quarter the vocabulary of the other students by the time they enter high school. At this writing, no national standards for preschool programs exist, and most programs are available only to parents who are able to pay for them. So, again, the children who need high-quality opportunities are the least apt to receive them.

We know that education is the answer to lifting children out of poverty and that when we do this, we improve the economy, lower crime, add value to people's lives, and strengthen our country. As teachers, we are in a unique position to make a difference and to change children's lives for the better, one classroom at a time.

8

Evaluating Learning With Authentic Assessments

Educators use grades primarily (1) for administrative purposes, (2) to give students feedback about their progress and achievement, (3) to provide guidance to teachers for instructional planning, and (4) to motivate students.

—Peter Airasian (1994)

Assessment has become an important topic in the last few years and not just because of the controversy about high-stakes tests and standards. Educators have come to realize that good assessment provides a wealth of information about the diverse learners in the classroom. Formative assessment allows us a peek at the prior learning of our students, the possible skill gaps, and the time needed by students to learn new information and processes. Assessment tells us, as teachers, whether the instructional practices we use in the classroom are working. Since 1998, when Black and William published their findings on formative assessment, educators have been discussing assessment in a new light. Black and William basically showed through empirical evidence that good formative assessment not only improves student success but to a degree higher than anything else accounted for educational interventions.

What is the difference then in formative and summative assessments? Popham (2008) uses the definition coined by the FAST SCASS committee of the Council of Chief State School Officers in a meeting in Austin, Texas, in October 2006. Here is their definition: "Formative assessment is a process used by teachers and students during instruction that provides feedback to adjust ongoing teaching and learning to improve students' achievement of intended instructional outcomes." Note that formative assessment is a process; it is not an end unto itself. Also of note is the fact that formative assessment informs both the teacher and the student as to where they are in terms of achievement.

USING FORMATIVE ASSESSMENT

As I stated before, formative assessment is a process, and it has as its goal to make the adjustments necessary either in the instructional program or by students to attain mastery of given instructional standards. Using formative assessment in the classroom allows teachers to determine the effectiveness of the instructional strategies that they are using. When those strategies are not working it provides an opportunity for teachers to make the necessary adjustments before students display failure. I include students because students need to be cognizant of their own progress and know when the methods that they are using for learning are not working. How do we make these important decisions?

Popham (2008) suggests that we use learning progression that is "a sequenced set of sub skills and bodies of enabling knowledge that, it is believed, students must master en route to mastering a more remote curricular aim." In other words, it is composed of the step-by-step building blocks students are presumed to need in order to successfully attain a more distant, designate instructional outcome. A learning progression starts with a target aim such as phonemic awareness. Reaching the target goal of achieving mastery might include such subskills as matching sounds, isolating sounds, blending, and so on. Brookhart (2001) says that an important part of formative assessment is giving students feedback. After all, one of the main purposes of formative assessment is to help both the teacher and the student to know what is working and what is not. The type of feedback and how it is given is important. We want students to know what they are doing well and what needs improvement. We want to enhance self-efficacy, not destroy it. We want students to feel in control of their own learning so just telling students what they did wrong is not very effective and may, especially with children from poverty, enforce the idea that they do not have control over what happens to them. Instead, we want to empower them by helping them to formulate a new plan based on the information provided. And, of course, the information should be in a format that makes sense to the student.

Summative assessment, on the other hand, is usually used to provide a grade or final progress report on student learning. High-stakes tests are a form of summative assessment that identify whether students have mastered the standards for their subject level and grade. Fisher and Frey (2007) provide this concise definition: "Summative assessments are typically used to evaluate the effectiveness of instructional programs and services at the end of an academic year or at a predetermined time. The goal of summative assessments is to judge student competency after an instructional phase is complete" (p. 4).

Assessment begins with effective planning on the part of the teacher and students. As teachers, we must ask ourselves what it is that we want students to know and be able to do as a result of the learning. Only then can we effectively plan our lessons. Lessons should begin with the end in mind. What is important for students to know and understand? Grant Wiggins and Jay McTighe (2005) describe a lesson design that looks at performance first. Before teachers build the lesson, they ask these critical questions:

- Which enabling knowledge (facts, concepts, and principles) and skills (procedures) will students need to perform effectively to achieve desired results? It is important to note here that how we teach declarative and procedural information is important as they are stored differently in the brain. If I want students to use vocabulary (knowledge) to complete a graphic organizer (procedural) it is important that the vocabulary has been taught in such a way that students can easily retrieve it to complete the process of a graphic organizer. I not only need to know which facts and which skills students need to know but how best to teach those.
- What activities will equip students with the needed knowledge and skills? How can I help students to make meaning from the knowledge and create mental models of the skills so that they can be used productively?
- What will need to be taught and coached, and how should it best be taught, in light of performance goals? In the diverse classrooms today, how I teach is as important as what I teach. Students are different in terms of the ways that they take in information and process and store it. I need to know my students so that I know the very best instructional practices that work for their culture.
- What materials and resources are best suited to accomplish these goals? Do I have the materials and resources needed for the success of my students, and will they make sense personally to the students that I teach?
- Is the overall design coherent and effective? How will I know if the teaching and learning are successful and if they're not, why?

In order to better assess how we teach and assess learning, let's look at what some of the experts are saying. Squires (2005) says that in a balanced curriculum teachers should ask the following questions about the tasks that students perform when thinking about how to assess (pp. 215–216):

- Does the significant task include an activity that can guide instruction?
- Does the significant task include language from the standards?

- Is the significant task description complex yet doable for most students?
- If students complete the significant task, will they understand the ideas, concepts, processes, and procedures from the standards embedded within the significant task?
- Will the significant tasks in the unit take (consume) 60 percent of the unit's allocated time?"

Assessment is built on declarative and procedural objectives written and provided to students prior to the lessons. Declarative and procedural objectives should be taught differently because they are processed differently in the brain and are stored (and retrieved) differently. We know from the research that intelligence is divided into two types. Intelligence in the form of knowledge such as facts, principles, and generalizations is sometimes called crystallized intelligence. Intelligence from cognitive processes is called fluid intelligence. Let's look at the two types of intelligences in light of how we teach.

DECLARATIVE INFORMATION

Declarative objectives are based on what students will know as a result of the teaching and learning process. Declarative objectives are factual and are taught with instructional tools different from procedural objectives. Declarative objectives are stored in a different part of the brain from procedural objectives. So it stands to reason that successful implementation and assessment must begin with the type of objectives being employed. Declarative objectives for a lesson on nouns and pronouns might look something like the ones shown in the box.

Declarative objectives: students will **know** the following:

- The definition of a noun
- The definition of a pronoun
- The rules for the use of a noun
- The rules for the use of a pronoun

For a lesson on shapes, the declarative goals might look like this:

Students will know the following facts:

- The vocabulary words associated with shapes (i.e., square, rectangle, circle, cone, triangle)
- The attributes of various shapes
- Why the study of shapes is important

Notice that all of the objectives are based on the students acquiring knowledge. They are not doing anything with the information at this point; they are gathering the facts that they will need to use the knowledge. Definitions, rules, and facts make up declarative objectives.

Assessing Declarative Knowledge

Most testing of declarative information is through what Stiggins (1994) calls *forced-choice assessment*. He defines forced-choice assessment as follows: "The respondent is asked a series of questions, each of which is accompanied by a range of alternative responses. The respondent's task is to select either the correct or the best answer from among the options. The index of achievement is the number or proportion of questions answered correctly."

Examples of forced-choice assessment include multiple-choice, matching, true-false, multiple-response, and fill-in-the-blank tests. My book *What Every Teacher Should Know About Student Assessment* (Tileston, 2004d) discusses these test types and provides an example for each.

We also assess declarative knowledge through questioning and other forms of dialogue with students or through students interacting with each other using techniques such as cooperative learning. Fisher and Frey (2007) warn that using questioning to determine understanding can be problematic. Why? If response time is not implemented equally, it can have a negative effect, or if the same students always answer then we are getting an incorrect idea about who really understands in the classroom. There is a big difference in knowing that six or seven students understand as opposed to knowing that all 32 understand. Fisher and Frey (2007) suggest that good questioning techniques are effective and provide these suggestions for using questions to gauge formative assessment:

- Choose good questions that identify the instructional purpose. Some questions require more than a yes or no response and some do not. Be aware of the level of learning required to answer your question.
- Present the question so that everyone knows the response format and then choose a respondent.
- Prompt student responses as needed. Pause after asking the question and after the student response.
- Provide immediate feedback to the student response. Provide an opportunity for the student to ask questions.
- Reflect on the results and make changes in the way that you ask questions based on the experience.

What if students respond incorrectly? Fisher and Frey (2007) make these suggestions:

- Cue: use symbols, words, or phrases to help student recall.
- Clue: use overt reminders such as "Starts with . . . ."
- Probe: look for reasoning behind an incorrect response or ask for clarity when the response is incomplete.

- Rephrase: pose the same question in different words.
- Redirect: pose the same question to a different student.
- Hold accountable later: later in the lesson, check back with the student who responded incorrectly to make sure that he or she has the correct answer. (p. 41)

PROCEDURAL KNOWLEDGE

Next, students need to know what they will do with these definitions, rules, and facts. These are the procedural objectives for the lesson. Procedural objectives, as the name implies, require the learner to employ a process to the learning. Procedural objectives for our lesson on nouns and pronouns might look like this:

Procedural objectives: students will be able **to do** the following:

- Distinguish between a noun and a pronoun
- Use the appropriate pronoun for the given noun
- Use capitalization correctly
- Write sentences using correct pronouns from a given prompt
- Write a paragraph using nouns and pronouns appropriately
- Justify their use of a pronoun from a given prompt
- Explain in their own words the difference between a noun and a pronoun

For our lesson on shapes, the procedural objectives might look like this:

Students will be able to do the following processes:

- Identify the various shapes from drawings
- Draw the shapes themselves
- Identify shapes from their surroundings; for example, windows, doors, and furniture

Procedural objectives take the knowledge of the declarative objectives to a more complex level, one at which the student demonstrates that he or she can use the information. When planning, the teacher asks, "What activities do I need to include in the lessons to determine that my students can use the information provided through the declarative objectives?"

Assessing Procedural Knowledge

In addition to the activities designed by the teacher to provide opportunities to use the declarative information, the following methods are often used to assess procedural knowledge.

Essays

Tileston (2004d) says, "The strength of essay-type assessments is in the stem for the essay itself. What do you want to know? Do you want to know if students understand the facts, or do you want to know if they can use reasoning, problem-solving techniques, or decision-making?" An example of an essay question that requires students to use higher-level thinking comes from the website of the Center for Research on Evaluation, Standards, and Student Testing (CRESST, www.cresst.org; see Figure 8.1).

Figure 8.1 Example of an Essay Question That Requires Procedural Knowledge

Since the start of the school year, your class has been studying the principles and procedures used in chemical analysis. One of your friends has missed several weeks of class because of illness and is worried about a major exam in chemistry that will be given in two weeks. This friend asks you to explain everything that she will need to know for the exam.

Write an essay in which you explain the most important ideas and principles that your friend should understand. In your essay, you should include general concepts and specific facts you know about chemistry, and especially what you know about chemical analysis or identifying unknown substances. You should also explain how the teacher's demonstration illustrates important principles of chemistry. Be sure to show the relationships among the ideas, facts, and procedures you know.

Short Written Responses

Tests that ask for short written responses are really a form of the essay but are limited to very specific information. These questions might only address declarative information, but they can address procedural information as well. The advantage to these types of tests is that, when carefully constructed, the questions test higher-level thinking. For example, for a short written response that tests only declarative information, elementary or middle school students might be asked to list the sequence of events in the chapter titled "Finders Keepers" from *Henry Huggins*, by Beverly Cleary. A procedural question might ask this: "In the story, the main character finds a dog that he wants to keep for his own. When the rightful owner shows up, our main character must make a decision. Make a list of possible solutions for the problem. Be sure to include at least three solutions that are your own ideas. Create a list of four criteria for making the decision about which of your options to use. Based on your criteria, which option will you chose? Defend your answer."

Oral Reports

Oral reports are an auditory form of the essay and may include both declarative and procedural information. According to Marzano (2000), their strength is in assessing topics that require information, thinking and reasoning, and communication skills.

Performance Tasks

Quality performance tasks can be an excellent way of assessing students' learning. However, performance tasks are often rote and low level. For this type of measurement to be useful, the task should reach higher levels of thinking and should require students to truly understand the topics studied.

All performance tasks, whether they are homework or independent projects, should include a matrix or rubric by the teacher so that students know exactly what is meant by a quality product. I also like to use a checklist for formative assessment feedback. For example, suppose a student is preparing a persuasive essay for class. I might provide a checklist on the important parts of the essay in advance so that the student will have no doubt as to my expectations for the essay. My checklist might look like Figure 8.2.

Figure 8.2 Checklist: Persuasive Essay

Parts (Essentials)	Points	Attributes (Qualities)
Thesis Statement		❑ Clear position taken ❑ Logical
Introduction		❑ Attention grabbing ❑ Thesis statement—last sentence
Voice		❑ Targets intended audience
Reasons		❑ Three reasons clearly stated in topic sentence(s) ❑ Emotion/logic based
Support/Elaboration		❑ Transition statements as links ❑ Supported with examples/other elaboration techniques ❑ Clinchers
Conclusions		❑ Restates position statement ❑ Reestablishes reasons ❑ Includes call to action

The persuasive-essay checklist provides talking points for the student and me as he or she creates the persuasive essay. I use a rubric for the final project that is also used as we dialogue throughout the process (see Figure 8.3).

Figure 8.3   Rubric: Persuasive Essay

Essay Rubric	Expert	Practitioner	Apprentice	Novice
Thesis	Clear and well stated: the three arguments are provided with supporting evidence	Clear: the three arguments may lack clarity as stated	Either not clear, or the three arguments lack clarity or evidence	Along with arguments and evidence, is either not there or does not make sense
Elaboration	Very colorful and interesting ideas for evidence presented in a logical format—many details	Some interesting details, needs more elaboration or logic	Limited use of descriptors; may lack clarity or logic	Limited or no use of elaboration or details
Conclusion	Follows the logic of the thesis and the evidence provided	Includes thought but does not follow the evidence precisely	Does not follow the logic of the thesis and evidence	Missing or not clear

The third part of the assessment process might be a student self-evaluation of the final product. I can use the original checklist and have the student show where he believes he did his best work and where he needs improvement.

Teacher Observation

We have focused so much on students feeling good about themselves that we have often been too positive or general in our praise. For teacher feedback to be effective, it must be specific, sincere, and both diagnostic and prescriptive. Let me show you what I mean. Saying "good job" to a student is not feedback. Feedback might sound something like this: "Jim, you have done a great job at writing your beginning goal for the learning. This has a personal interest for you. Now, think about why we might spend time at school on this topic. Why would it be important for people to know in life? How might you use this information in other situations? How will this help you to be a better citizen? Family member?"

In most instances, declarative objectives are taught before the procedural objectives. The declarative objectives provide the scaffolding for the procedural. These goals should be provided to students visually. For older students, put the goals up in the room and refer to them often. Goal setting is an important part of the teaching-learning process. Refer to the goals frequently so that students can measure their own learning. For young students, put the goals up using visual symbols. Also, send the goals home to parents so that you have a baseline of support for what you are trying to accomplish with the class. Ask students to write personal goals for the learning. In Chapter 1, we discussed why the learning must have personal meaning to our students. Personal meaning is a brain-friendly way to tap into the self-system of the brain. Authentic assessment looks at both declarative and procedural objectives.

Rubrics and Matrices

The next step in authentic assessment is for the teacher to provide to the students the criteria for success. This might be in the form of a rubric, matrix, or written steps. Except with very young children, this information should be written and in the hands of every student. The rubric alone is a form of self-assessment for the students, since they should be given opportunities to refer to it often to determine how well they are learning. For the lesson on nouns and pronouns, the rubric might look like Figure 8.4.

Figure 8.4   Rubric for Nouns and Pronouns

Great Job	You Are on Your Way	Not There Yet
1. The student understands the vocabulary words and can state them in his or her own words.	1. The student can recite the vocabulary words and definitions but has difficulty putting them into his or her own words or defending the definitions.	1. The student has merely memorized the vocabulary and definitions. There is little if any understanding or ownership to them.
2. The student understands the rules and attributes that identify a noun and a pronoun and can use those rules to create and use his or her own nouns and pronouns for writing.	2. The student knows the rules and attributes of both the noun and pronoun but still struggles at times to remember some of the rules.	2. The student cannot appropriately use the rules for the noun and pronoun consistently.
3. The student demonstrates an understanding of the mechanics of using nouns or pronouns correctly by supplying the correct form in given prompts. The student can defend in his or her words the rules that are employed.	3. The student demonstrates an understanding of the mechanics of using nouns and pronouns most of the time with some prompting but may not be able to defend his or her choices consistently.	3. The student demonstrates a surface knowledge of the use of nouns and pronouns but can only use them correctly with prompting by the teacher.

Note that in the rubric provided in Figure 8.4, Items 1 and 2 relate to the declarative information while the rest of the items relate to the processes employed using the declarative information. So often, assessment is limited to declarative objectives. By deliberately writing the objectives as both declarative and procedural, we are more likely to assess both.

Anything for which we are taking a grade or making an assessment should have criteria that are given to the students up front, before the assignment—even homework. This takes the "gotcha" out of assessment. Figure 8.5 is an example of a matrix for mathematics homework, which was originally published in my book *What Every Teacher Should Know About Student Assessment* (Tileston, 2004d).

> Anything for which we are taking a grade or making an assessment should have criteria that are given to the students up front.

Figure 8.5 Matrix for Nouns and Pronouns

Criteria	Attributes
All problems worked	• Steps followed correctly • All work shown • Work is checked
Understanding of mathematics is evident	• Explains work thoroughly • Is able to justify answers • Is able to explain the process to others
Work is turned in at a timely interval	• Work is on time • Work is complete
Work is legible	• Work is neat and legible • Work can be easily seen and understood

MEASURING SUCCESS

Good assessments, whether formative or summative, reflect both declarative and procedural information. To create quality formative and summative assessments, schools must ask some hard questions about the assessment. Does the assessment provide adequate information about the degree of learning? What is the appropriate vehicle for the assessment? Has adequate time been allowed to ensure that assessment of long-term memory is taking place, not just memorization for the short term? What is important to measure? Do we need to measure the process, the product, or both? More important, does the assessment truly reflect the learning? Is it more important that students are able to name the date of the Yalta Agreement or that they know the process to find that date, should they need it?

Assessment should be an active demonstration of students' understanding and their ability to apply this understanding. Good formative assessments have, as their goal, to inform both teachers and students about the effectiveness of the teaching/learning process and where changes need to be made. We need to know that students can construct meaning from the learning. In my book *What Every Teacher Should Know About Student Assessment* (Tileston, 2004d), I paraphrase Wiggins and McTighe (1998), who say that when students truly understand, they can

- explain in their own words,
- interpret by reading between the lines to give additional and plausible information,
- apply by transferring information from one format or situation to another,
- see in perspective by justifying a position as a point of view,
- demonstrate empathy for others' points of view,
- and reveal self-knowledge by identifying their own ideas, feelings, strengths, and weaknesses.

We discussed in Chapter 5 the importance of setting high expectations for student products. The teacher needs to set the standard high and give specific parameters for the expected project. While it is important to give students choices, it is equally important to set parameters to ensure that the final product reflects quality. Instead of saying to students that we want a research project on the brain and learning, we might say instead that we want a research project on the brain and learning that includes, at a minimum, the work of Jensen and Sousa. We might also let them choose the format of the finished product. For example, the finished product might be written as a monograph on the need for changes in education, presented in a multimedia format using PowerPoint, or dramatized as a student forum. Students have choices, but the teacher sets the parameters for the level of quality. The highest level a product can attain is that of providing usefulness beyond the person who created it. Figure 8.6 shows indicators that will be present when authentic assessment is practiced.

Figure 8.6 Indicators That a Variety of Assessments That Authentically Evaluate the Learner Are Used

Assessment Tool	Indicators of Success
Student products	Demonstrate understanding by being able to use the learning in different contexts
Student products	Indicate student use of a variety of inquiry skills to solve problems, create products, and access information
Student assessments	Indicate a wide range, reflect the learning, and follow the rubric
Student assessments	Indicate learning beyond state and national standards
Formative assessments	Provide feedback to both the teacher and the students on what is working and what is not

CONCLUSION

There is no way that we can teach students everything they need to know in order to be successful. First of all, we don't know what will be necessary for them to know in their lifetimes to be successful. We must give them tools to formulate understanding, structures for problem solving, and research retrieval skills, and then we must assess to see if they can use these tools. We do this by giving them assessment exercises that employ those processes. Independent projects, experiments, and complex problem solving are some of the ways this can be accomplished.

If assessment is authentic, it should be closely aligned to the day-to-day experiences of the curriculum and should inform our decisions. Try using the following questions (Tileston & Darling, 2008a, p.150) to authentically assess student learning:

- Does the unit contain clear outcomes, appropriate for the student audience, that describe the learning expectation? (expectations)
- Are these outcomes drawn from specific state or national standards? (expectations)
- Are the instructional strategies that were chosen effective for the concepts and processes stated in the learning expectations? (learning)
- Will the student activities, assignments, and learning experiences that provide the opportunity to learn the outcomes provide adequate time and practice with available options for differentiation? (learning)
- Are all of the outcomes adequately addressed in the activities, assignments, and learning experiences, with none left out? (learning)
- Are all of the outcomes, or learning expectations, assessed appropriately? (assessments)
- Is the means of assessment (e.g., multiple choice, essay, rubrics, performance tasks, and so on) appropriate for assessing both kinds of knowledge with options for differentiation? (assessment)
- Is the language of the assessment the same as that used in instruction? (assessment)
- Is the number of items or tasks appropriate for the significance of the content and processes being measured, as well as the length of time spent in teaching and learning them? (assessment)

9

Encouraging In-Depth Understanding With Real-World Applications

Since our brain is designed to learn for survival, it is very good at learning that which it perceives to be useful, practical, and real.

—Eric Jensen (1997)

We live in an age of a vast amount of information that is changing at warp speed. We cannot possibly teach students everything they will need to know to be successful because we don't even know what that is. Thanks to exponential advancements in technology, all of us are having difficulty keeping up with the changes taking place in our students' lives today—much less tomorrow. The role of the classroom teacher has evolved from the "sage on the stage" to the collaborative participant and leader of learning taking place in the classroom. We cannot adequately prepare students for the jobs they will have because, as Marc Prensky (2006) points out, our students will have seven professions in their lifetime, and five of those don't even exist today.

When I was in school, many of the diseases and problems that we face today had not even been envisioned. My teachers could not teach me about diseases such as AIDS; what they could do was provide me with the in-depth skills needed to make informed decisions. There is no way that we can teach students everything that they will need to know in life. That is not to say that we should not teach students factual information; declarative information is critical to the basics of education. What I am saying is that students need to know how they learned the information and how to apply the processes of learning so that they can transfer those processes to real-world issues throughout their lives. In Chapter 3, a model for a KNLH chart is provided. The *H* in the chart stands for "How did I learn?" Students need to realize which processes were utilized to learn material. Information does not become a part of long-term memory until we believe that we know it.

Jensen (1997) lists four stages of understanding: starter knowledge, relational knowledge, globalized knowledge, and expert knowledge. Using Jensen's four stages as a basis, let's examine each and the processes that lead to students becoming experts in the learning.

STAGE 1: STARTER KNOWLEDGE

The starter knowledge stage of learning is sometimes referred to as surface knowledge. Students are memorizing facts that may or may not have any specific meaning to them. For example, students may be learning the components of the periodic table in science, the definitions of shapes in mathematics, the reasons for World War II in history, or the sequence of events in a story. This type of information is usually assessed by paper-and-pencil tests where students merely prove that they have memorized the information. The real-world application is low at best, and more often students are not even aware of how they learned the information or of the application to the real world. Rote memorization is only effective when the answer is always the same, such as multiplication facts, and the information must be revisited periodically or it will be lost. Marzano (2001a) says that in the knowledge domain, the lowest levels of learning are vocabulary terms, facts, and time sequences.

STAGE 2: RELATIONAL KNOWLEDGE

In the relational knowledge stage of the learning, students are making connections across disciplines and time. When they study the reasons for World War II, they are looking for patterns that cause conflicts and analyzing current world situations for similarities. Instead of just learning the names and dimensions of shapes, they are finding those shapes all around them. They no longer look at a story for its parts but for patterns that can be applied to other situations. Dr. Seuss's *Sneeches* is not just a funny story about fuzzy green animals with stars in the middle of their stomachs but comments on a pattern of behavior (prejudice, exclusivity) that occurs in life. The conflicts in *Hamlet* are a picture of similar conflicts that occur throughout history.

Marzano (2001a) discusses comprehension in the cognitive system as "responsible for translating knowledge into a form appropriate for storage in permanent memory" (p. 33). He uses two processes to explain comprehension in his new taxonomy. Synthesis is the first of the processes. When students synthesize they are able to take knowledge down to its key characteristics. They understand the critical attributes. The other process that identifies comprehension is representation. Representation is the nonlinguistic way in which the new information is viewed. Graphic organizers are an example of representation.

STAGE 3: GLOBALIZED KNOWLEDGE

Students who participate in globalized knowledge understand the impact of the knowledge beyond their immediate world. They understand the impact on their community, country, world, and planet. At this point, the learning takes on a more in-depth, personal meaning as students examine their own belief systems and how they feel about the issues involved. This type of learning is more likely to stay with the student throughout life—not just for the test on Friday. They see things from other points of view and have a better understanding of the value of the information and processes that they have acquired. Marzano (2001a) discusses knowledge utilization as the stage in which students can use the information in a useful way such as decision making, problem solving, experimental inquiry, or investigation. These are all processes that require understanding of the information learned and the ability to analyze.

Students who can make decisions can use the knowledge gleaned to choose from alternatives the one best solution for them for the problem at hand. They have the ability to weigh possibilities and to determine whether some options carry more weight than others.

Students who problem solve have the ability to accomplish a goal in spite of obstacles or limiting conditions. One of the main differences in problem solving and decision making is that problem solving involves making decisions when there are obstacles while decision making does not. Students who use experimental inquiry are able to test and generate hypotheses that are realistic and sound.

In the example in Figure 9.1, students can fully answer the question, "Now what?"

"What?, So What?, and Now What?" is a reflection exercise that helps students think about the learning and its usefulness to them personally and beyond. The "What?" stands for "What have you learned?" Students list facts and ideas that have surfaced as a result of the learning. The "So What?"

Figure 9.1   What?, So What?, and Now What?

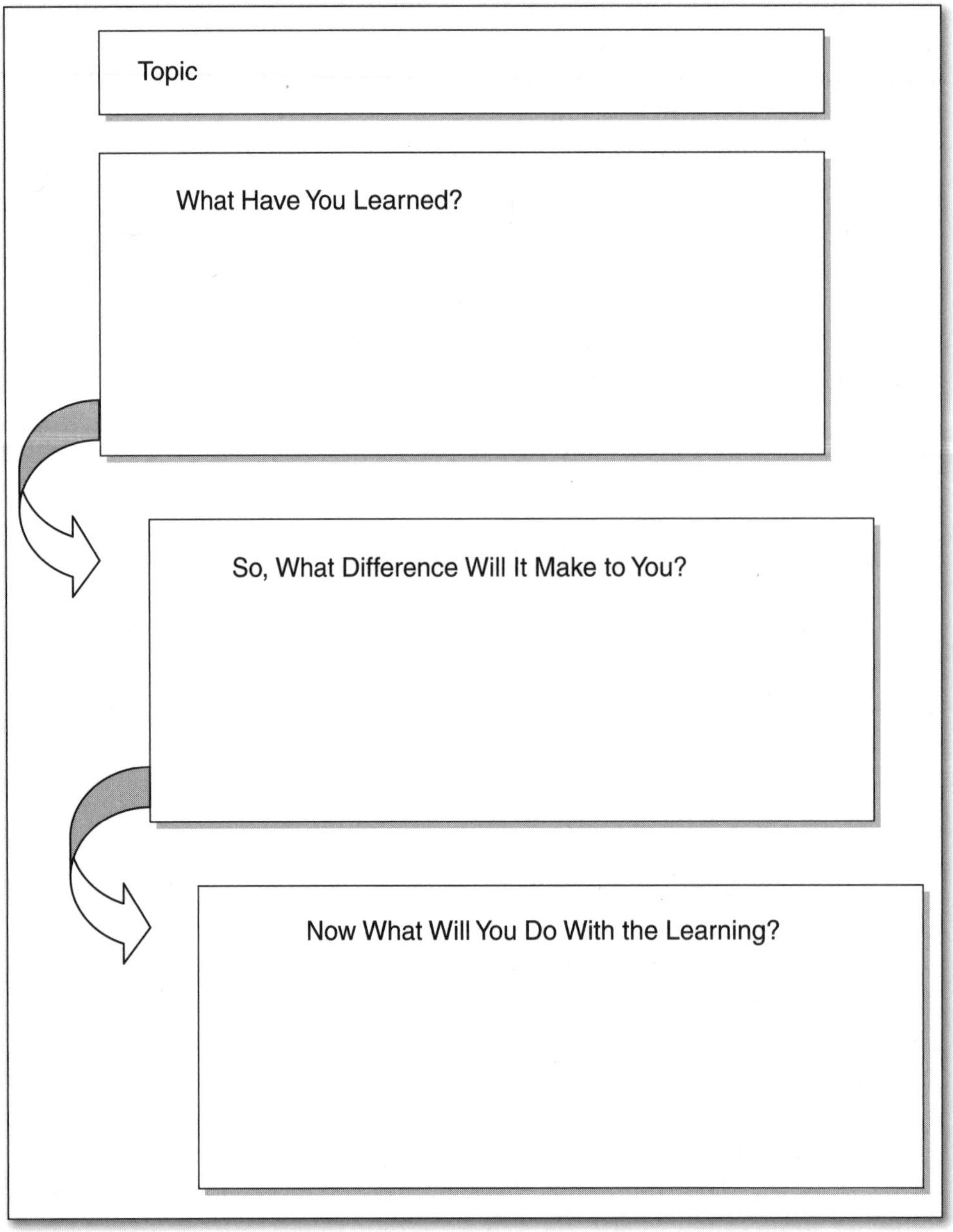

Topic

What Have You Learned?

So, What Difference Will It Make to You?

Now What Will You Do With the Learning?

stands for "So, what difference will it make to you?" Students write, in their own words, the personal application of the learning to their lives. The "Now What?" stands for "Now what will you do with the learning?" At this stage, students look beyond the present to how the information might be used in the future and beyond themselves. They must be able to make connections to complete this part of the exercise. Reflection is an important part of any lesson, because until students believe that they have learned, the learning will not be real to them. Wiggins and McTighe (2005) say that students at this stage can see perspectives.

STAGE 4: EXPERT KNOWLEDGE

Students at the expert knowledge stage are insightful and can apply the information in a variety of contexts. They employ all six of the facets of understanding provided by Wiggins and McTighe (2005). They can do the following:

- Explain what they know in their own words. Students not only explain in their own words, but, as this ability is developed, they can justify their interpretations. They will have the ability to decide what the underlying problem or central fact is. They will also be able to predict, based on fact. Figure 9.2 is a graphic organizer that I use to teach students to be able to make good predictions. In this figure, students are given basic facts and information and then asked to make a prediction about what will happen next. Notice that their predictions must be based on facts and that they have to be able to justify the facts.

Figure 9.2   Prediction Tree

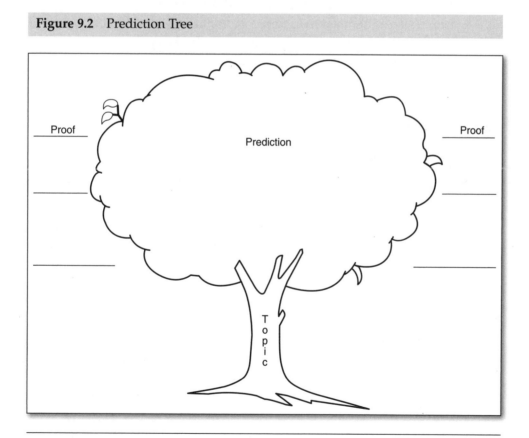

When students are able to make accurate predictions, they can do the following:

- Interpret information and processes, including hidden meanings. At a higher level, these students can "read between the lines and offer plausible accounts of the many possible purposes and meanings of any text (i.e., book, situation, or human behavior)" (Wiggins & McTighe, 2005).
- Apply information in real-world contexts. The student can project the information into a variety of contexts other than the classroom.
- See their own perspective and the perspective of others. This includes critiquing information for its worth. Wiggins and McTighe (2005) say that the student with expert knowledge can also do the following:
  - Know the limits as well as the power of an idea
  - See through argument or language that is biased, partisan, or ideological
  - See and explain the importance or worth of an idea
- Demonstrate empathy for the ideas and assumptions of others. The learner truly understands the motivations and views of others even when the learner does not agree with those ideas.
- Understand themselves in terms of prejudices, understandings, and limitations. The learner participates in thinking about the learning and self-assessing accurately. An expert learner will have the ability to accept feedback and put it to use.

SERVICE LEARNING AS A REAL-WORLD EXPERIENCE

Last year I visited Istanbul where I met with teachers and students as we talked about twenty-first-century skills. All students in the school system that I visited are required to complete a service learning project by sixth grade. The project is a learning experience about issues and/or problems outside of their own school and home. The issues can involve the community, Istanbul, the country, or anywhere in the world. Students not only study the issues but create solutions as well. Four years ago while in the Netherlands to speak to educators from all over Europe, I was taken with the service learning projects that were featured and that had won international awards. These students are making a difference in the world. More and more service learning is becoming a priority in this country as well. The website www.servicelearning.com offers wonderful ideas and step-by-step processes for schools that want to make service learning an integral part of the curriculum. It really is taking the classroom to the real world. Here are some examples of the projects from schools in the United States as found on the service learning website.

Examples of Service-Learning

- Elementary children in Florida studied the consequences of natural disasters. The class designed a kit for families to use to collect their important papers in case of evacuation with a checklist, tips about rescuing pets, and other advice to make a difficult situation easier, which students distributed to community members.

- Middle school students in Pennsylvania learned about the health consequences of poor nutrition and lack of exercise and then brought their learning to life by conducting health fairs, creating a healthy cookbook, and opening a fresh fruit and vegetable stand for the school and community.

- Girl Scouts in West Virginia investigated the biological complexity and diversity of wetlands. Learning of the need to eliminate invasive species, the Scouts decided to monitor streams and presented their findings to their Town Council to raise awareness of the issues concerning local wetlands.

- University students in Michigan looked for ways to support struggling local nonprofit organizations during difficult economic times. Graduate communication students honed their skills while providing a wide variety of public relations services with community partners, including developing press kits and managing event coordination.

While we always want to encourage students to volunteer in their communities, this website makes a distinction between acting as a volunteer to serve the community and actually participating in a service learning project with the emphasis on learning. Here is how they define the difference:

> If school students collect trash out of an urban streambed, they are providing a service to the community as volunteers; a service that is highly valued and important. On the other hand, when school students collect trash from an urban streambed, then analyze what they found and possible sources so they can share the results with residents of the neighborhood along with suggestions for reducing pollution, they are engaging in service-learning." (Learn and Serve, n.d.)

CONCLUSION

In a classroom where real-world application to the learning is actually applied, there will be evidence in the lesson that the knowledge has been connected to authentic situations that occur outside the classroom as well as within. Moreover, students will be given opportunities to reflect on the learning as evidenced by journals and written guided reflections. Depth of understanding will be evident through journals, products, and written materials, and a part of assessment will be the student's ability to tie the learning to real-world situations.

Figure 9.3 shows the indicators that will be present when real-world application is applied to the learning. Students will be able to make the transition from surface knowledge to more complex thinking and to make use of the domains of knowledge discussed. Their use of knowledge will go beyond the boundaries of the classroom and themselves to the real world.

Figure 9.3   Indicators That Instruction Promotes Real-World Application of the Learning

Assessment Tools	Indicators of Success
Lesson plans	Indicate that the knowledge has been applied to authentic situations that occur outside the classroom as well as within
Journals and student products	Indicate depth of understanding and opportunities for reflection
Assessments	Indicate students' understanding of real-world application
Service learning	Indicates that students are learning and at the same time using what they have learned to make others' lives better

10

Integrating Technology Seamlessly Into Instruction

Our educational system is running like a fine Swiss watch. The problem is that there is very little market today for fine Swiss watches.

—David Thornburg

Students enter our school hallways each day fresh from a digital world that not only allows them to communicate throughout the world, but also gives them the ability to solve problems, do research, and perform at levels never before available. Students today are not just using technology, they are creating it. You need only go to one of the many communication sites to see videos, pictures, and music created by students and shared on these sites. Those same students often go to classrooms where the primary learning tools are lecture, note taking, and rote learning: tools that do not provide opportunities for them to interact with the learning. No wonder they drop out mentally. Interactive technology is the tool of the twenty-first-century classrooms just as a pen, pencil, blackboard, overhead, and slates were tools of past centuries. It should be an integral part of the classroom experience, not an add-on that students use once a week in a lab. One of the problems is that this is the first generation in history to master the tool of the classroom before the teacher. As has often been noted, students today are digital natives—they were born into a world of multimedia and speak digital as their first language. Most of us were paper trained and speak digital as a second language—and we will never be able to speak digital without an accent.

In the preceding chapters, nine best practices were discussed. All of these practices can be greatly enhanced with the use of appropriate technology. As a matter of fact, technology is the vehicle that can help shift classrooms to best practices.

LEARNING ENVIRONMENT

In Chapter 1, climate and its powerful effect on student learning were discussed. Through the use of technology, teachers will more effectively be able to monitor and provide anytime, anywhere assistance to students. Through Internet and intranet resources, students are able to get assignments, additional help, and clarifications online. Students who are absent or unable to attend classes can learn online. Students have more choices as a whole world of learning opportunities becomes available. High school students can receive their diploma online through rigorous and creative programs that are not limited by walls or the availability of courses, but allow students to take the courses they want and need from their laptops. Being able to take French from a teacher in France and having the opportunity to practice with students who speak the language fluently gives new life to learning other languages. Telementoring will be the wave of the future as students are linked to adults with like interests and abilities through web experiences. For those of us who were "paper trained" rather than growing up with technology, there are some simple ways to get started using technology as a tool in the classroom.

- Ask students to write papers using Microsoft Word and submit them to you in that format so that you can use the tracking system to make comments and to show students what they need to change, revise, or elaborate. Students then use the tracking to answer your questions and to make the necessary changes. It is exactly the way that I work with my editors when I write books for publication.
- Use websites that allow you to set up chat rooms just for your students to discuss the material presented and to provide feedback to each other. One website, http://pbworks.com, allows the teacher to set up the site with a password only known to his or her students.
- Use instant-messaging programs such as iChat for text conversations between students or between students and the teacher.
- Take advantage of video conferencing or online programs such as www.gotomeeting.com that allow you to communicate with your students outside of the classroom.

Using technology as a tool is brain friendly because it reflects what students do outside of the classroom. Students should not have to "power down" when they come to school. As I've noted elsewhere (Tileston, 2004d), there are basic good-practice reasons to incorporate technology into your teaching:

- Technology is not limited by the classroom walls.
- Technology does not know or care what the student's socioeconomic status may be and thus helps level the playing field for these students.
- Technology provides an equal opportunity for everyone to learn.
- Technology is more in tune with the way our students today learn.
- Technology is so much a part of the real world that to limit its use in the classroom is to limit our students' ability to compete in the world.

DIFFERENTIATION

In Chapter 2, the need to address the various learning styles of students was outlined. Much software is available to the classroom today that incorporates visual, verbal, and kinesthetic learning. Software tools allow the teacher who is unfamiliar with visual models to create them easily and effortlessly just by plugging in his or her teaching outline. Students who need visuals to learn and those who are dyslexic and need graphic representations will be able to view the learning in a format that is comfortable and meaningful to them. Lessons can be more interesting with the addition of multimedia formats that more closely mirror the world from which our students come.

Many teachers today use interactive whiteboards, and that is certainly a step up from the overheads and chalk boards of the past because students can interact with them as they do on a daily basis outside of school with their other technology devices. NBC.com offers video clips that can be used in the classroom without worry about breaking copyright laws. These clips have a wealth of use in a classroom filled with visual learners. How exciting to show students the landing on the beach in Normandy rather than merely reading or talking about it. Today's learners want to see the learning first; then they will explore additional reading or discussion as they need it (Jukes, McCain, & Crockett, 2010). This is very different from my generation who read first and then looked at charts and graphs to gain more information. This is the generation that learns a new video game by playing it first, and then if they need further information, such as how to get to the next level, they call a friend or go online for "cheat notes."

PRIOR KNOWLEDGE

In Chapter 3, I discussed the need to help students make connections from prior learning to the new learning. Through technology, students will be able to view the learning as well as hear it. They will also have the opportunity individually to review past information. Through the use of animation and visuals, teachers will be able to give the learning relevance to a degree not possible in the past. Talking about polar bears to children who live in southern regions has much less relevance than taking them through virtual classrooms to a zoo or a region where they can see real polar bears.

Technology opens up a whole new world of learning to those students who need visual representations. I recently volunteered to read to a group of first graders in a school near me. When the teacher brought the children to the library for the lesson, she sat one child off to the side by himself. She whispered to me that he would probably not sit quietly for the lesson and that she was placing him so that she could easily remove him from the room if necessary. Instead of just reading the book to the children, as we so often do, I read the book as I showed selected pictures from the story using PowerPoint software and an LCD projection device that showed the pictures from my computer on a television monitor. Not only did the young man in question sit quietly for the story, but when I had finished, he yelled, "Do it again!" This was a visual child in an auditory world, and he had already become a discipline problem in first grade because he was being forced to learn in a modality not comfortable for him.

Most students today are visual and kinesthetic—after all, they have been looking at and interacting with technology all of their lives. Jukes, McCain, and Crockett (2010) remind us that there is a vast gap between how those of us who speak digital as a second language prefer to teach and how digital learners prefer to learn. Digital learners prefer the following:

1. Receiving information quickly from multiple multimedia sources while we may prefer a slow and controlled release of information from limited sources

2. Processing pictures, sounds, color, and video before text while we tend to provide text before pictures, sounds, video, and color

3. Random access to hyperlinked multimedia information while we tend to provide information linearly, logically, and sequentially

4. To network simultaneously with many others while we want students to work independently before they network and interact

5. Instant gratification with immediate and deferred rewards while we tend to defer gratification and defer rewards (p. 36)

Marc Prensky (2006) says that by the time our students are 21 they will have played video games for more than 10,000 hours, sent and received more than 250,000 e-mail and text messages, talked on the phone 10,000 hours, and watched more than 20,000 hours of television. They will have spent considerably less time in school. From this information it is easy to see where the influences on youth today rest.

Here are some sites specifically to help teachers as they work with the digital generation:

- www.sitesforteachers.com
- http://teachers.teach-nology.com
- www.theteacherlist.ca

LONG-TERM MEMORY

In Chapter 4, the need to help students put the information into long-term memory rather than just memorizing for a test was addressed. The sensory devices that are a part of technology will allow teachers to enrich their lessons for the classroom. Research projects have greater relevance when students encounter information and concepts through virtual classrooms, distance learning, the Internet, and worldwide e-mail. Student projects take on a new dimension with technology as their guide. Semantic memory will be enhanced by technology because relevance or meaning will be more evident as students are able to apply information to authentic situations and problems. Student projects can be created virtually so that immediate relevance is seen rather than having to wait until a time in the future as students might have to do later when they have jobs that deal with real problems.

Teachers can enhance episodic memory by using technology to create props or tools that trigger recall. Ask students to create their own book of sounds; have students go to www.clipart.com to add pictures of things that start with particular letters. Pitler, Hubbell, Kuhn, and Malenoski (2007) also provide these recommendations for adding nonlinguistic representations. For student and teacher presentations check out the following:

- Project-based learning with multimedia at http://office.microsoft.com/en-us/help/HA011411961033.aspx
- Educational PowerPoint templates at www.paducah.k12ky.us/curriculum/PPoint/
- PowerPoint in the classroom at www.actden.com/pp
- Keynote user tips at www.keynoteuser.com/tips/index.html
- Keynote theme park for free theme downloads at www.keynotethemepark.com/index.html
- Animation ideas at http://webmonkey.com
- Animation factory at www.animationfactory.com/help/tutorial_gif.html

HIGHER-LEVEL THINKING

In Chapter 5, the importance of teaching to higher-level thinking in the classroom was reported. Technology assists with this by providing a rich environment for learning. The possibilities are limitless. Let your students become adept at claymation through this website that teaches students to combine claymation and PowerPoint to create powerful presentations: www.pendergast.k-12.az.us/advisorservices/as/wow/claytutorial.pdf. By using good productivity tools, the quality of products that students can produce is enhanced. Written reports take on a new dimension when the student is able to add animation and other visuals in a PowerPoint or similar presentation. An added bonus is that, with technology, students can work on their project anytime and anywhere rather than having to rely on the office hours of libraries or museums. A group of high school students used technology to study the force of motion on roller coasters by setting up their rides and then measuring the g-forces. Some other sites to get you started in high-level thinking include the following:

- Learn to create and use WebQuests at http://webquest.org
- Instant projects at http://instantprojects.org
- Skill-building activities at www.iknowthat.com
- Visuals at http://www.brainpop.com
- Secondary skills at www.explorelearning.com
- Inventive thinking at www.bkfk.comCollaboration

In Chapter 6, the need for collaboration was emphasized. Technology opens all the windows and doors to make this possible. Students use social networking daily; it is time that we took advantage of this form of technology in the classroom. Parents may not be able to come to the school, but the school can come to them through e-mail, the Internet, distance learning, and virtual classes. Schools can communicate better with all of the stakeholders through virtual opportunities. Student projects and studies will not be limited to the students in the classroom. Students can work with other students in the building and in other schools as well. Teachers can communicate with each other literally anytime and anywhere. Collaboration takes on a whole new meaning with technology. Students can use www.calendars.net to create class calendars for activities and projects. Teachers, students, and parents can communicate together at www.globalschoolnet.org/GSH or create online learning communities at http:moodle.org. They can use http://delicious.com to keep favorite websites, music, books, and so on together and to share with other students.

BRIDGING THE GAPS

The need to reach 100 percent of students was revealed in Chapter 7. Technology is the tool that will lead the way toward making education equitable for all students, regardless of their background. The computer does not see race, wealth, gender, or beliefs: it is a great equalizer, especially when students have equal access to computers. Parents from poverty may have more access to technology than their kids, since computers are often available to them at work while they are not available at home. However, if we accept the predictions of technology writers such as Jukes and Prensky, computers will soon (in the next five years or so) be so economical that everyone will have one. Actually, phones today provide a usable method for students to use the web and to communicate with anyone and are certainly coming down in price. The hidden agendas of society are not a factor there. Schools that need and want to bridge the gap should be actively pursuing the resources to make high-level technology possible. Governments that tout high standards must come to realize that high standards require high-level tools. The future of education rests on two things: first, quality teachers who not only can teach in the traditional classroom but also in a nontraditional setting and who can inspire; second, high-level technology that mirrors the real world. These are the gateways to produce a quality product.

ASSESSMENT

The authentic assessments in Chapter 8 take on a higher level of quality when we add productivity tools. Students will also be able to create electronic portfolios and logs that help track and showcase growth. An electronic portfolio is probably a better tool for university and job applications than the traditional test scores and grades. If completed properly, the portfolios show the multiple talents of the individual rather than the single ability to take tests. Use websites that provide surveys to find out the background knowledge of your students. Some of these include the following:

- Create surveys at www.surveymonkey.com
- Get your survey on the web at www.policat.com
- Create rubrics at http://rubistar.4teachers.org and http://edweb .sdsu.edu/webquest/rubrics/weblessons.htm
- Create your own blog at www.blogspot.com, or better yet, let students create the blog and keep parents and other students informed about the exciting things going on in your classroom

Nothing is more real-world than the experience of being in the place discussed, conversing with the people being studied, or watching practitioners use the skills being learned. Through video conferencing, virtual classrooms, distance learning, and the Internet, all of these things are possible today.

MEASURING SUCCESS

Schools that place a priority on technology provide technology that is accessible to everyone, all day, not just in laboratory situations. Both instructional technology, which deals with creating an optimum teaching and learning environment, and educational technology, which deals with technology literacy, are a vital part of the curriculum. Emphasis is on using productivity tools, not expensive drill-and-practice software, and student products reflect the use of those tools.

At a minimum, these schools provide access to the Internet, intranet, and communication devices for teachers and students. Students learn processes that reflect technology use at a high level. Classes will not be limited to a single space or single building but will be opened up to the possibilities of distance learning. Through technology, students will be able to take classes never before possible. The lines between high school and college will be blurred as students take college and career courses along with their basic-skills classes for high school graduation. As teachers learn and are trained online, it only follows that students will turn more and more to online learning opportunities, and within this decade schools may take on a completely different role as students learn virtually.

Figure 10.1 shows the indicators that will be present when technology is utilized at a quality level.

Figure 10.1 Indicators That Technology Is Used at a Quality Level

Assessment Tools	Indicators of Success
Observation	Technology tools will be accessible to everyone.
Observation	Technology will be integrated into the classroom, not relegated to an isolated lab setting.
Student products	Indicate an emphasis on productivity tools, not expensive drill-and-practice software
Technology tools	Indicate that students and teachers have access to the world
Student products	Indicate learning processes that reflect technology use at a high level
Parent surveys	Indicate access to school Internet and intranet services to retrieve information from student assignments, progress, and curriculum anytime
Field trips	Reflect virtual trips to places heretofore not accessible to the school
Class offerings	Indicate that they are not limited by a single space or building, but offer possibilities through the worldwide web
Student products	Will indicate that students have been taught the elements of information retrieval, including the ability to discern between primary and secondary resources, the difference between fact and opinion, and the ethics of using technology responsibly
Lessons	Indicate the use of technology to make them more dynamic, emotional, and relevant
Technology in general	The technology of the present will be used as a tool just as we used pencils and pens in the past.

CONCLUSION

Through technology, the classroom takes on another dimension: the world—rather than the bricks-and-mortar building—becomes the classroom. Resources never before possible, relevance and depth of study at a level never before achieved in a classroom, and the exchange of ideas with unlimited possibilities boggle the mind. Technology is not an end in itself; it can lead us toward the type of classroom of which we have all dreamed.

These are not ideas for the future—I do not consider myself to be a futurist. These are the possibilities of now. Education should be so exciting, so exacting, that students would literally run to get to it. Technology will help make this a reality.

11

Putting It All Together

Thomas Friedman has been quoted as saying, "When I was growing up, my parents told me, 'Finish your dinner. People in China and India are starving.' I tell my daughters, 'Finish your homework. People in India and China are starving for your job.'"

—Daniel Pink (2005)

The 10 teaching practices offered in this book are only a beginning—but an important beginning. They provide a framework for classroom instruction that is very different from the instruction of the past centuries. This is not merely a change in teaching strategies, but a whole new way of looking at the learning process. We have never had so much information available to us before on how the brain works. We also have never had as many challenges before us as we do in today's very diverse surroundings. The classroom teacher has taken on roles beyond teaching. I often tell teacher groups that if all there was to teaching was just knowing our subject matter and providing it to students, we would not have a teacher shortage in any field.

In an article for *Newsweek*, Anna Quindlen (2004) lamented the fact that the war on poverty is far from won, citing Census Bureau figures showing that for the third year in a row the number of Americans living below the poverty line had increased. She is quick to point out that the poverty line was set quite low—at $18,000 per year for a family of four. "When you adjust the level to reflect reality, you come closer to 35 percent of all Americans who are having a hard time providing the basics for their families, what the Community Service Society of New York calls 'The Unheard Third.'"

As you look for solutions to your school's problems and as you work to incorporate the ideas from this book, the following checklist may be of help to you. It is offered as a guide for schools as they begin to look toward ways to not only narrow the achievement gap but to close it.

Across the country:

- Be cognizant of the attitudes and plans of lawmakers and political candidates in regard to poverty.
- Be an informed voter.
- Work for an alignment of federal and state resources to help the poor and to level the educational playing field.
- Be proactive in assuring that federal and state measures for success (i.e., testing) are free of bias or restrictions that single out any particular group.
- Work for national standards that take into account all students and that provide the resources for success—not just for the more affluent areas but for all students and teachers.
- Volunteer to serve on boards and committees, especially those that are setting policies for testing and for resources.

In your community:

- Become proactive in the community to provide better health, mental, mentoring, physical, and fiscal resources for your students.
- Work with parents and other caregivers for solutions.
- Actively involve parents and members of the community in advisory groups.
- Set meetings at times that working parents can attend.
- Use technology to help parents and other stakeholders stay informed.
- Provide interpreters for parents who do not speak English.
- Take into consideration that some parents have come from countries where those in authority have not been fair or friendly. They may be wary of school personnel, especially if they are not citizens.
- Provide opportunities for your students to become proactive in their own communities with projects that include such activities as art, music, writing, starting a newsletter, and providing help at clinics or other community facilities.
- Because poverty is a matter of a lack of resources, help students increase the resources within their own communities.

In your school:

- Make good nutrition a priority and fight for offerings in your school that don't just look good but taste good as well. Good lunches in the trash can don't help anyone.
- Emphasize good hydration for learning.
- Examine curriculum and books for examples of bias and work toward a plan for eliminating bias throughout the school.
- Set norms that include the respect for all people.
- Prove that you believe all kids can learn.

- Set norms that say learning is important.
- Provide advisory groups that include students as well as community people.
- Provide opportunities for afterschool activities.
- Provide opportunities for additional resources that are a part of the school budget, such as nurses, counselors, and librarians.
- Make sure that the resources in your school are rich in culture and that they reflect the races and ethnicities of your students. While Martin Luther King Jr. Day is important, it should not be the only time of the year that we celebrate diversity.
- Be aware of students who are absent too much, are in danger of dropping out, in danger of failure, and so forth. Provide an adult advocate for every student in the school. (This can be done through teams of teachers and senior students.)
- Fight for better conditions for your school if they are not up to par with other schools in your region.
- Be proactive in asking for the resources that your students need to be successful.
- Provide ongoing professional development that includes ways to reach students in your school and that examines the best practices, especially in regard to brain research and learning.

In your classroom:

- Set classroom standards with your students that define expectations that all students will be respected.
- Bond with all of the students through trust and feedback.
- Create relationships first.
- Be aware of the culture of your students; do not expect students to be like you.
- Model the behavior that you expect of your students.
- Provide information to your students about resources available to them.
- Make your students aware of the need for good nutrition and hydration in regard to learning.
- Communicate caring and concern for all students, but remember that it is not our sympathy they want but a quality education.
- Communicate high expectations while keeping the threat level low.
- Provide scaffolding so that students can learn at a high level.
- Help your students understand how their own brains work and how that affects all that they do.
- Have, as your goal, to build resiliency in your students from poverty.
- Build positive self-efficacy in your students.
- Provide a variety of teaching resources in the classroom that take into account the backgrounds, ethnicity, socioeconomical status, and culture of your students.
- Use a variety of modalities in the classroom, especially visual and kinesthetic.
- Contextualize the lessons.

- Create experiences that help students make connections between prior learning and experiences and the new learning.
- Create opportunities for students to set personal goals for the learning.
- Explicitly show students how to use self-talk and other techniques to revise their goals when they encounter problems.
- Help students complete work at a quality level.
- Provide specific and prescriptive feedback on an ongoing basis to students.
- Teach in a variety of ways so that students learn in the way to which they are accustomed.
- Help students make the transition from the language of the street to the language of the classroom.
- Provide opportunities for students to work together in heterogeneous groups.
- Emphasize the gifts that all students bring to the table.
- Recognize and overcome linguistic bias.
- Recognize and overcome stereotyping bias.
- Recognize and overcome exclusion bias.
- Recognize and overcome fragmentation/isolation bias.
- Recognize and overcome selectivity bias.
- Recognize and overcome unreality bias.

In addition, provide opportunities for networks with other teachers in your building and in other schools to support and encourage you.

Stalin supposedly said that he did not need armies to take over countries. He said to give him the country's children for one generation, and he would have the country. Who has greater influence over society than teachers? Our influence has the power to change a new generation—for the better.

References

Airasian, P. (1994). *Classroom assessment* (2nd ed.). New York: McGraw-Hill.

Arroyo, C. (2008, January). *The funding gap 2007.* Washington, DC: Education Trust.

Association for Supervision and Curriculum Development. (1999). *ASCD yearbook.* Alexandria, VA: Association for Supervision and Curriculum Development.

Benard, B. (2003). Turnaround teachers and schools. In B. Williams (Ed.), *Closing the achievement gap: A vision for changing beliefs and practices* (2nd ed., pp. 115–137). Alexandria, VA: Association for Supervision and Curriculum Development.

Black, P., & William, D. (1998). Inside the black box: Raising standards through classroom assessment. *Phi Delta Kappan, 80*(2), 139–144, 146–148.

Booth Sweeney, L. (2001). *When a butterfly sneezes: A guide for helping kids explore interconnections in our world through favorite stories.* Waltham, MA: Pegasus.

Brookhart, S. M. (2001). Successful students' formative and summative uses of assessment information. *Assessment in Education, 8*(2), 153–170.

Choiniere, R., & Keirsey, D. (1992). *Presidential temperament: The unfolding of character in the forty presidents of the United States.* Del Mar, CA: Prometheus.

Clauss-Ehlers, C. S. (2006). *Diversity training for classroom teaching: A manual for students and educators.* New York: Springer.

Clayson, M. (2007). *Human memory pathways.* Available online at http://ezinearticles.com/?Human-Memory-Pathways&id=461184

Corbin, B. (2008). *Unleashing the potential of the teenage brain: 10 powerful ideas.* Thousand Oaks, CA: Corwin.

Covey, S. R. (1989). *Seven habits of highly effective people.* New York: Simon & Schuster.

Diamond, M. C., Scheibel, A. B., Murphy, G. M., Jr., & Harvey, T. (1985). On the brain of a scientist: Albert Einstein. *Experimental Neurology, (88),* 198–204.

Doidge, N. (2007). *The brain that changes itself: Stories of personal triumph from the frontiers of brain science.* New York: Penguin.

Duckworth, A. L., Peterson, C., Matthews, M. D., & Kelly, D. R. (2007, January). Grit: Perseverance and passion for long-term goals. *Journal of Personality and Social Psychology, 92,* 1087.

Fisher, D., & Frey, N. (2007). A tale of two middle schools: The difference in structure and instruction. *Journal of Adolescent and Adult Literacy, 51,* 204–211.

Fitzgerald, R. (1996). Brain compatible teaching in the block schedule. *The School Administrator, 8*(2), 20.

Gardner, H. (1993). *Frames of mind: The theory of multiple intelligences* (2nd ed.). London: Fontana.

Gibbs, J. (1994). *Tribes.* Santa Rosa, CA: Center Source.

Glasser, W. (1994, March–April). Teach students what they will need in life. *ATPE News,* 20–21.

Goleman, D. (1995). *Emotional intelligence: Why it can matter more than IQ.* New York: Bantam Books.

Hanson, J. M., & Childs, J. (1998). Creating a school where people like to be. *Educational Leadership, 50*(1), 14–16.

Henderson, N., & Milstein, M. (2003). *Resiliency in schools: Making it happen for students and educators.* Thousand Oaks, CA: Corwin.

Individuals with Disabilities Education Improvement Act of 2004. Pub. L. No. 108-446, 118 stat. 2647 (2005).

Jackson, R. R. (2009). *Never work harder than your students & other principles of great teaching.* Alexandria, VA: Association for Supervision and Curriculum Development.

Jacoby, P. (1991). *Region XIII Education Service Center.* Austin, TX: Region XIII Education Center.

Jensen, E. (1995). *The learning brain.* Del Mar, CA: Turning Point.

Jensen, E. (1997). *Completing the puzzle: The brain-compatible approach to learning.* Del Mar, CA: Turning Point.

Jensen, E. (1998). *Introduction to brain-compatible learning.* Del Mar, CA: Turning Point.

Jensen, E. (2003). *Tools for engagment: Managing emotional states for learner success.* Thousand Oaks, CA: Corwin.

Jensen, E. (2006). *Enriching the brain: How to maximize every learner's potential.* San Francisco: John Wiley and Sons.

Jensen, E. (2010). *Different brains, different learners: How to reach the hard to reach* (2nd ed.). Thousand Oaks, CA: Corwin.

Jukes, I., McCain, T., Crockett, L. (2010). *Understanding the digital generation: Teaching and learning in the new digital generation.* Thousand Oaks, CA: Corwin.

Keefe, J. M. (1997). *Instruction and the learning environment.* Larchmont, NY: Eye on Education.

Kinneavy, J. L. (1991). Rhetoric. In J. Flood, J. M. Jensen, D. Lapp, & J. R. Squire (Eds.), *Handbook of research on teaching the English language arts.* New York: Macmillan.

LAB at Brown University. (2001). *The diversity kit.* Providence, RI: The Education Alliance.

Learn and Serve. (n.d.). *What is service learning?* Available online at http://service learning.org/what_is_service-learning/service-learning_is

Lipsey, M. W., & Wilson, D. B. (1993). The efficacy of psychological, educational, and behavioral treatment. *American Psychologist, 48*(12), 1181–1209.

Long, L. (2006). *Painless algebra* (2nd ed.). Hauppauge, NY: Barrons Educational.

Marzano, R. J. (1992). *A different kind of classroom: Teaching with dimensions of learning.* Alexandria, VA: Association for Supervision and Curriculum Development.

Marzano, R. J. (1998). *A theory based meta-analysis of research on instruction.* Aurora, CO: Mid-Continent Regional Educational Laboratory.

Marzano, R. J. (2000). *Transforming classroom grading.* Alexandria, VA: Association for Supervision and Curriculum Development.

Marzano, R. J. (2001a). *Designing a new taxonomy of educational objectives.* Thousand Oaks, CA: Corwin.

Marzano, R. J. (2001b). *What works in schools.* Alexandria, VA: Association for Supervision and Curriculum Development.

Marzano, R. J. (2007). *The art and science of teaching: A comprehensive framework for effective instruction.* Alexandria, VA: Association for Supervision and Curriculum Development.

Marzano, R. J., Norford, J. S., Paynter, D. E., Pickering, D. J., Gaddy, B. B. (2001). *A handout for classroom instruction that works.* Alexandria, VA: Association for Supervision and Curriculum Development.

Marzano, R. J., & Kendall, J. S. (2008). *Designing and assessing educational objectives: Applying the new taxonomy.* Thousand Oaks, CA: Corwin.

Mid-Continent Research for Education and Learning. (2002). *Explorers through time.* Available online at http://www.mcrel.org/PDF/Curriculum/5011CM_Explorersthroughtime.pdf#search=%22explorers%20through%20time%22

Newmann, F. W., & Wehlage, G. G. (1993). Five standards of authentic instruction. *Educational Leadership, 50*(7), 8–12.

No Child Left Behind Act of 2001, 20 U.S.C.

O'Neil, J. (1995). On lasting school reform: A conversation with Ted Sizer. *Educational Leadership, 52*(5), 12.

Parks, S., & Black, H. (1992). *Organizing thinking* (Vol. 1). Pacific Grove, CA: Critical Thinking Press.

Pink, D. H. (2005). *A whole new mind: Moving from the informational age to the conceptual age.* New York: Riverhead Books.

Pink, D. H. (2009). *Drive: The surprising truth about what motivates us.* New York: Riverhead Books.

Pitler, H., Hubbell, E., Kuhn, M., & Malenoski, K. (2007). *Using technology with classroom instruction that works.* Alexandria, VA: Association for Supervision and Curriculum Development.

Popham, J. W. (2008). *Classroom assessment: What teachers need to know* (5th ed.). Boston: Pearson.

Prensky, M. (2006). *Don't bother me Mom—I'm learning.* St. Paul, MN: Paragon House.

Quindlen, A. (2004, September 20). The last word. *Newsweek, 68.*

Rank, M. R. (2005). *One nation, underprivileged.* New York: Oxford University Press.

Renzulli, J. S., & Reis, S. M. (2008). *Enriching curriculum for all students* (2nd ed.). Thousand Oaks, CA: Corwin.

Sousa, D. (2005). *How the brain learns.* Reston, VA: National Association of Secondary School Principals.

Sousa, D. (2006). *How the brain learns* (3rd ed.). Thousand Oaks, CA: Corwin.

Sprenger, M. (1999). *Learning and memory: The brain in action.* Alexandria, VA: Association for Supervision and Curriculum Development.

Sprenger, M. (2002). *Becoming a "wiz" at brain-based teaching.* Thousand Oaks, CA: Corwin.

Squires, D. A. (2005). *Aligning and balancing the standards-based curriculum.* Thousand Oaks, CA: Corwin.

Stiggins, R. J. (1994). *Student-centered classroom assessment* (2nd ed.). Columbus, OH: Merrill.

Tileston, D. W. (2004a). *What every teacher should know about effective teaching strategies.* Thousand Oaks, CA: Corwin.

Tileston, D. W. (2004b). *What every teacher should know about learning, memory, and the brain.* Thousand Oaks, CA: Corwin.

Tileston, D. W. (2004c). *What every teacher should know about media and technology.* Thousand Oaks, CA: Corwin.

Tileston, D. W. (2004d). *What every teacher should know about student assessment.* Thousand Oaks, CA: Corwin.

Tileston, D. W. (2005). *The ten best teaching practices: How brain research, learning styles, and standards define teaching competencies* (2nd ed.). Thousand Oaks, CA: Corwin.

Tileston, D. W. (2006). *Strategies for active learning.* Thousand Oaks, CA: Corwin.

Tileston, D. W. (2010). *What every teacher should know about diverse learners.* Thousand Oaks, CA: Corwin.

Tileston, D. W., & Darling, S. K. (2008a). *Teaching strategies that prepare students for high-stakes tests.* Thousand Oaks, CA: Corwin.

Tileston, D. W., & Darling, S. K. (2008b). *Why culture counts: Working with children from poverty.* Bloomington, IN: Solution Tree.

Tileston, D. W., & Darling, S. K. (2009). *Closing the poverty gaps.* Thousand Oaks, CA: Corwin.

Toliver, K. (1993). *Good morning, Miss Toliver.* [PBS Video Series]. Washington, DC: PBS.

U.S. Census Bureau. (2006). *Income, poverty, and health insurance coverage in the United States: 2005.* Accessed at www.census.gov/prod/2006pubs/p60—231.pdf on May 23, 2008.

U.S. Department of Health and Human Services. (2001). *Mental health: Culture, race and ethnicity—A supplement to mental health: A report of the Surgeon General.* Rockville, MD: U.S. Department of Health and Human Services. Public Health service. Office of the Surgeon General.

U.S. Department of Labor. (1991). *Scans: Blueprint for action.* Washington, DC: Author.

Walker, D. (1998). *Strategies for teaching differently: On the block or not.* Thousand Oaks, CA: Corwin.

Wang, M. C., & Kovach, J. A. (1996, 2003). Bridging the achievement gap in urban schools: Reducing educational segregation and advancing resilience-promoting strategies. In B. Williams (Ed.), *Closing the Achievement Gap* (pp. 10–36). Alexandria, VA: Association for Supervision and Curriculum and Development.

Werner, E. E., & Smith, R. S. (1992). *Overcoming the odds: High-risk children from birth to adulthood.* Ithaca, NY: Cornell University Press.

Whisler, N., & Williams, J. (1990). *Literature and cooperative learning: Pathway to literacy.* Sacramento, CA: Literature Co-op.

Wiggins, G., & McTighe, J. (1998). *Understanding by design.* Alexandria, VA: Association for Supervision and Curriculum Development.

Wiggins, G., & McTighe, J. (2005). *Understanding by design* (2nd ed.). New York: Prentice Hall.

Zeichner, K. M. (2003). Pedagogy, knowledge, and teacher preparation. In B. Williams (Ed.), *Closing the achievement gap: A vision for changing beliefs and practices* (2nd ed., pp. 99–114). Alexandria, VA: Association for Supervision and Curriculum Development.

Index